Samantha Babington has beeing
with a Diploma in Life Coac   the
Coaching Academy (Europe   ing
college) in 2005. She also works as a Speech and Language
Therapist (having gained a BSc in Clinical Language Sciences
from Leeds Metropolitan University) and has a wealth of
experience working in the educational sector in both the UK
and New Zealand. She currently works within the NHS
helping adults and teenagers with special needs in East
London.

SERENDIPITY'S SECRET

*A Novel Way to Achieve your Dreams and Find
the Path to Happiness*

Samantha Babington

Best Wishes

Samantha Babington

Book Guild Publishing
Sussex, England

First published in Great Britain in 2010 by
The Book Guild Ltd
Pavilion View
19 New Road
Brighton, BN1 1UF

Typeset in Janson by
YHT Ltd, London

Printed in Great Britain by
CPI Antony Rowe

A catalogue record for this book is available from
The British Library.

ISBN 978 1 84624 456 8

Praise for *Serendipity's Secret*

'If you don't believe that a cat can show you the way Home, you haven't met Serendipity! Thank you Samantha Babington for this charming and insightful tale of self-discovery.'

Susan Jeffers, Ph.D., bestselling author of
Feel the Fear and Do it Anyway and *Embracing Uncertainty*

'I like this book's approach very much – friendly, with substance....'

Tal Ben-Shahar, New York Times bestselling author of
Happier – Learn the Secrets to Daily Joy and Lasting Fulfillment

'This book is excellent and hits the mark very well ... a very thoughtful and persuasive book, which I hope is very widely read. It deserves to be.'

Dr Anthony Seldon, Master of Wellington College,
and prolific author

'This is a delightful book; wise, uplifting and touching. Read it for pure enjoyment and learn how to reach your goals!'

Sandra Howard, bestselling novelist

'Great and innovative – I really enjoyed reading it!'

Lorraine Thomas, Chief Executive of The Parent Coaching Academy and bestselling author of *The 7 Day Parent Coach*

'*Serendipity's Secret* is an enchanting book that teaches great life wisdom in an inspiring and fun way. A must-read for life coaches and anyone seeking to improve their life and develop their intuition.'

Brian Mayne, author of *Goal Mapping* and *Sam the Magic Genie*

This book is dedicated to my late great uncle,
His Honour Judge Anthony Babington, who overcame
seemingly insurmountable obstacles in order to achieve
his dreams

Contents

Preface

When I decided to write a self-help book I was faced with the dilemma of exactly how to go about it. However, as a qualified life coach, I knew I wanted to write something that would clearly illustrate the amazing power of life coaching and the incredible results that can be achieved. I also wanted my book to be innovative and entertaining as well as practical and, above all, something that would instantly uplift the spirits of whoever read it.

Looking for inspiration, my eyes were drawn to my mother's cat, Pepsi, who was sitting in her basket by the window. It occurred to me that she now spent most of her life sitting in that basket and I felt a little sad as I remembered how young, sleek, sprightly and interactive she used to be. I couldn't help but wonder when it was *exactly* that she had lost her zest for life. It then dawned on me that it was about the same time that she had been given her comfy new basket! My eyes were then drawn to a framed poster on the wall with a picture of a cat above the words 'Everything I learned about life I learned from my cat'. It was at that moment the idea for my book was born. I would write a self-coaching guide based around a story, which would make the benefits of life coaching accessible to everyone. My heroine would be a cat who is stuck in a rut and has long given up on her dreams and aspirations. Yet, she still secretly harbours one kittenhood dream; that of seeking out the legendary 'Celestial Dairy' where she can drink the 'Cream of Life' and all her wishes will come true. This looks set to remain just a dream until she encounters a mysterious life coach who claims to be able to help her.

Having decided on a premise for my book I now just needed a name for my cat!

Days went past trying to think of something suitable until one day, out of the blue, a word sprung into my head. The word was 'Serendipity'. At this point I wasn't *totally* sure what the word meant – I just knew it was what I wanted to call my cat. I then went to find a dictionary, my fingers crossed, hoping that the word would mean something appropriate to my book. I then had my answer. The dictionary defined 'serendipity' as the effect by which one accidentally discovers something of value, often while looking for something else. Researching the origin of the word I found it derives from an old Persian fairy-tale, *The Three Princes of Serendip*.

This story tells of three men who were always finding wondrous treasures while searching for other things. In my story, Serendipity finds the true meaning of happiness while searching for the Celestial Dairy.

Having decided on a cat called Serendipity, I then had to find a character to coach her. By chance, the same evening I was flicking through a TV guide and my eyes were drawn to a film with the title *Pollyanna*. The film was based on the book *Pollyanna* by Eleanor H. Porter which tells the story of Pollyanna Whittier, a young girl who goes to live with her wealthy Aunt Polly after her father's death. Pollyanna's philosophy of life centres around what she calls 'The Glad Game' where she always tries to find something to be glad about in every situation. With this philosophy, and her own sunny personality, she brings so much happiness to her aunt's dispirited New England town that she transforms it into a pleasant, happy place to live. Again, I had my answer. Serendipity would be coached by a parrot, and her name would be Pollyanna. It then occurred to me that stumbling upon this name was a perfect example of serendipity!

Finally, in terms of metaphors, the Celestial Dairy is where you harbour your hopes and dreams; the Cream of Life is the happiness you can acquire when you get there; the comfortable warm basket is the Comfort Zone that often holds you back; Pollyanna is your Higher Self, the part of you that is filled with wisdom, creativity and courage; Serendipity is the luck you find when you listen to your Higher Self and begin to take action.

Acknowledgements

First and foremost, many thanks to all my family for their help and encouragement while writing this book.

To the Coaching Academy for their invaluable support and advice throughout my journey to becoming a life coach.

To Colin for lending me his house in Paraparaumu, New Zealand, while I wrote the last few chapters of this book.

To Steve in Tauranga, New Zealand, for his support during and after my training to be a life coach.

Lastly, to my mother's cats Pepsi and Mischief for their constant inspiration!

1

'When the pupil is ready, the teacher will appear'[1]

Serendipity the cat yawned a big wide yawn. As she slowly opened her eyes, her thoughts turned to the day ahead.

From where she was sitting, she had a good view out of the window and could see that the sun was shining. That was good, as it meant she could sit in her basket and soak up the sun's warm rays. She hoped it would stay sunny all day as that would mean she wouldn't have to get up at all.

She considered what an excellent sun trap her basket was on days like these. In fact, her basket was warm and comfortable on any day of the year, whatever the weather was like outside. Yes, it was comfortable even on days when it was cloudy, wet, windy or even snowing!

You see, it really didn't matter at all to Serendipity what the weather was like – because she never went outside.

Not ever.

Well, not for the past two years anyway.

Not since she had been given her comfortable, warm basket.

Yes, there was a time when she had gone out and had fun with the other cats that lived in the lane. Yet, now she had become accustomed to the comfort and security of her basket, she really didn't bother to go out any more.

---

[1] Zen proverb.

1

Besides, from where her basket was situated by the window in the conservatory, she still had a good view of the world outside.

She could see the colours of the garden below and watch the changing of the seasons. She could take in the rows of fields beyond that stretched out as far as the eye could see and wonder what might lie beyond the furthest hills. She could see her owners come and go, watch children playing in the field and spy on the many cats who lived in the lane.

There was Ginger, the large tom cat, who guarded his territory ruthlessly, growling and hissing at any cats who dared to cross his path. There was Snowy, the show cat, proudly showing off her pure white coat to anyone who chose to look. There was Tabby, the athlete, who entertained the crowd with his amazing acrobatic feats, fearlessly leaping from roof to roof without so much as a blink of the eye. There was Smudge, and her partner Spot, who were so in love, content to spend their days cuddled up together under their favourite rhododendron bush.

Not that Serendipity knew their real names but it was fun to watch and pretend that she knew. Watching their lives played out via her seat in the window, these cats seemed like movie stars to her, each appearing truly blessed in some way or another.

Sometimes she would wonder what it would be like to be part of that world outside – but only *sometimes*.

After all, she had everything she wanted inside this room. She had her comfortable warm basket with its familiar smell, her food in the bowl next to her, her water that was always fresh and her litter tray that was always emptied.

Yes, that was indeed enough for Serendipity!

Well, all she really did was eat and sleep, so what else did she need anyway?

No, this was her life and had been for the past couple of years, so she really couldn't complain.

Of course, there were times when she caught herself feeling bored, lonely or frustrated, as each day seemed to merge meaninglessly into the next.

When this happened, she would remind herself that many cats didn't have a nice warm basket, regular meals, nice clean water and a litter tray. She reminded herself that some cats had to sleep out in the cold and fend for themselves. They had to catch their own food and find their own shelter. Just imagine what sort of life that would be!

With that thought Serendipity shuddered, snuggled deeper into her nice warm basket and again considered the day ahead.

Right, so what shall I do today? she asked herself.

To help her decide, she carefully weighed up the options.

1. *Sit in her basket and soak up the sun.*

That sounded good! Yes, she would definitely do that, as long as the sun stayed out of course.

2. *Look out of the window.*

Yes, she could definitely do that too, whatever the weather!

3. *Sleep.*

Always a good option!

4. *Catch some mice.*

Although that was her 'official' job, it would mean getting out of her basket. Besides, she was no good at mousing anyway. So, not such a great option.

5. *Eat at least three meals.*

3

Yes, that sounded promising! She only wished the food wasn't always the same. Tuna with jelly.

Although she liked tuna with jelly, she wished she could have something else *occasionally*. Like, perhaps, tuna with gravy, or perhaps salmon with gravy, or even something that *wasn't fish*!

Or even perhaps something like ... *cream.*

Yes, she could really do with some of that! Even just a *little* cream to take away the taste of tuna.

As her thoughts turned to cream, she considered how that would really make her day. She imagined how wonderful the cream would taste, its silky texture on her tongue and the smooth liquid melting down her throat.

Yes, how amazing indeed that would feel!

With these thoughts fresh in her mind, she again looked out of the window at the garden, to the fields and hills beyond which stretched out as far as the eye could see.

As she took in the scene before her, she could feel herself slowly drifting off into a blissful sleep, still deep in her thoughts of cream.

Yet, as her eyes began to slowly close, something in the distance caught her attention.

She wasn't sure what it was exactly, but she didn't think it had been there a moment ago. As she focused hard on the horizon, she thought she could just make out something rising from behind the furthest hill.

But what could it be?

As her eyes began to adjust, she realised that it looked like smoke gently rising up to form a strange pattern in the sky. But where could the smoke be coming from and why was it rising like that from behind the hill?

As she pondered these questions she again felt sure it had never been there before. Or maybe, just maybe she had just never *noticed* it before?

She considered this was certainly not part of her usual routine, looking at strange smoke and thinking of cream! There was definitely something fishy in the air – and it sure wasn't tuna!

Just then, another thought occurred to her. She didn't really dare consider the possibility. Yet the thought filled her with a strange feeling and one which she hadn't experienced for a long, long time.

The feeling was quite odd. It started at the pit of her stomach and moved in a strange flutter up her body.

There was one possibility that had started this feeling. It was only a small possibility but it *was* a possibility all the same.

Could that smoke be coming from ... the Celestial Dairy?

When Serendipity was growing up she had often heard about the Celestial Dairy. It was a story that had been passed down from generation to generation, so most cats had heard about it. Yet, sadly, many dismissed it as nothing more than a rural myth.

Yet, as a kitten, the story had filled Serendipity with such wonder and excitement that she was determined to believe the story was true, even if no one else did!

The story went that somewhere, far, far away, there was a dairy located on a magical farm. Yet, only those cats who dared to seek it out could come and live there. These cats were brave indeed, having found the courage to embark on such a long and perilous journey. Those who managed to reach the Dairy were granted their heart's desire and a never-ending supply of cream.

But this wasn't any old cream.

No, *this* was the 'Cream of Life'. This cream tasted so wonderful and was so magical that anyone who drank it would be ensured a life of eternal happiness.

Yet, over the years, Serendipity had lost faith in the story of the Dairy and had begun to think that maybe it *was* just an old cat's tale after all. But now, as she looked out of the window to the fields beyond, she remembered being told that smoke rising from behind the furthest hill was a signal, for those who dared, to come and seek the Dairy out.

Could there really be something in the story after all?

As she considered this possibility, she thought to herself, *I wonder what it would be like to live at the Celestial Dairy and to drink the Cream of Life and . . . what on earth would I wish for if I did get to drink it?*

As she struggled to think of something she would wish for, it began to dawn on her that there was really little point in wishing for anything at all. The Celestial Dairy was so far, far away and, after all, she would have to leave her basket that was so warm and comfortable.

It was a waste of time even thinking about getting there. Why get her hopes up only to be disappointed?

Serendipity suddenly felt angry for kidding herself for one small moment that her life could be any different. No, she would have to stay where she was and make the most of the tuna and jelly she knew would be served up, predictably, in about an hour.

Just enough time for another nap, she thought, and off she dozed dreaming of . . . cream.

2

'Hope is the thing with feathers that perches in the soul, and sings the tune without the words, and never stops at all'[2]

Serendipity woke up with a start. She wasn't sure what had woken her but she knew she must have slept for over an hour as the sun was now much higher in the sky. *Feeding time*, she thought, with a mixture of anticipation and indifference. She casually looked over at her bowl and to her surprise saw it was still empty.

But how could that be?! Why on earth was her bowl still empty? She should definitely have some food by now! Not that she was really *that* hungry but ... she *always* had food in the morning ... and ... after all ... eating it *was* a way to kill some time.

As she pondered the empty bowl and the absence of food, out of the corner of her eye she noticed something else highly unusual. On the table, in the middle of the room, was a strange parcel, and on the side of the parcel were the words:

TEACHER'S PET STORE

Although it was an unusual-looking parcel and looked quite out of place, Serendipity hoped that it was something nice for her. It was such a big parcel that maybe, just maybe it was a

---

[2] Emily Dickinson (poet, 1830–1886).

new, *even more comfortable* basket (if indeed it was possible to find something more comfortable than her current basket!).

As Serendipity pondered this thought, she felt herself drift off once again into a blissful sleep, dreaming of her new, more comfortable basket. She could smell the familiar scent, feel the warmth surrounding her, and she felt so safe and secure ...

When she finally awoke, Serendipity yawned and noticed that the sun was now even higher in the sky. She guessed it must be around midday.

Surely I must have some food by now! she thought impatiently.

She slowly turned her head towards the bowl, but again, to her surprise, saw that it was still empty. *Never mind*, she thought, *I still have my nice new basket to look forward to – much more exciting than a boring old bowl of tuna!*

Yet, when she turned her head, full of anticipation, towards the table, to her surprise and disappointment she saw that the parcel was no longer there.

Where's my new basket? she thought with great irritation.

So curious was Serendipity to find out where it had gone that, despite the considerable effort involved, she climbed out of her basket and sauntered into the hall.

There were two rooms leading off from the conservatory. One led to the study and the other to the main living room. The only time she went into either room was when she was told to catch a mouse – which luckily wasn't that often.

Which room should I try first? she thought.

She then considered it didn't really matter which room she tried first, as long as she found her new basket.

Serendipity could see that the door to the living room was already slightly ajar. So, with her nose pressed firmly against the door, she began to nudge it open.

When she had opened it wide enough to squeeze through, she cautiously entered and looked around the room. To her disappointment she saw that there was nothing unusual about this room and *definitely* no basket in sight.

OK, then I guess it must be in the study, she thought, and ambled out of the room, feeling increasingly irritated by this inconvenience.

Nudging the door to the study, it appeared to be firmly closed. Yet, with a few more pushes from her nose, Serendipity slowly managed to prise it open. As she looked around the room, this time she *did* notice something out of place.

Next to the window was a brand new table, and on that table was something that, to her dismay, was definitely *not* a new basket. Instead, it appeared to be some enormous metal contraption with heavy bars. In fact, it looked much more like a prison cell than a comfortable warm basket.

To make matters worse, in that metal prison was what appeared to be some sort of a *bird*. But the bird was definitely *not* like the ones she used to chase around the garden. No, this bird was big, and brightly coloured, with a large beak, large claws and . . . it was staring right at her!

Serendipity was filled with a mixture of fear and anger. *Who was this strange creature and where was her new basket?*

Not sure what to say or do, she stood frozen to the spot. *Should she run and hide or should she stay and find out where her new basket was?*

While her mind raced with these thoughts, the silence was suddenly broken by a voice coming from inside the cage.

'Hi, I'm Pollyanna – but you can call me Polly. Pleased to meet you.'

Serendipity looked up at the bird with a mixture of surprise and shock.

What on earth should she say to this strange creature?

'I'm . . . I'm Serendipity,' she eventually stammered. *But I'm not pleased to meet YOU,* she thought.

'Serendipity, that's a nice name,' the bird replied cheerily. 'So, how are you today?'

'Well, I was fine until you turned up,' spat Serendipity, not really sure what to say, yet sure that this bird was in some way responsible for losing her basket, taking her food and generally ruining her day.

'I had my whole day planned out and now you've ruined it,' she added, flicking her tail with fury.

'So, what were your plans?' Polly enquired, showing no sign of being at all bothered by the accusations fired at her.

Serendipity took in a deep breath to quell her anger. 'Well, I was going to ... ah, eat my food and, well, lie in the sun, and sleep ... and ... ' Serendipity paused as she struggled to outline her day in a way that would sound at all interesting to the bird.

'And what else?' asked Pollyanna, gently preening her feathers.

'Well, er, lots of things,' Serendipity replied, still feeling a little lost for words. 'Like, well ... just things!'

'So how have I ruined things for you?' Pollyanna asked matter of factly.

'I don't know ... ah ... you ... well, you just have,' replied Serendipity defiantly, feeling she really didn't need to explain herself to this stranger.

'Oh dear, that's a shame,' said Polly, somewhat dismissively while continuing to preen her feathers.

There was then a long silence when neither bird nor cat said a word.

Serendipity was seething.

Who did this bird think it was coming into her home and ruining her day?! And how dare it question her in this manner!

Yet, despite her anger and disappointment in not finding her new basket, she couldn't help but be a little curious as to who this bird was and why it had turned up at her house that day.

Serendipity had often been told that curiosity killed the cat. Yet, despite this warning, she figured as cats were supposed to have nine lives, she probably still had several left. Besides, she didn't really feel like she had lived even one *full* one yet.

With that in mind, it was Serendipity who finally broke the silence.

'So, who are you anyway?' she asked, sounding rather too interested for her liking.

'I'm a parrot,' replied Polly matter-of-factly.

Serendipity remembered once hearing a story about a parrot when she was a kitten. Yet she had to confess to still knowing nothing much about them.

'Well, what sort of parrot?' she enquired, trying not to sound *too* interested this time.

'A very special sort of parrot. Or so I've been told!'

'What makes you so special?' Serendipity asked suspiciously.

'Well, for a start, I help make dreams come true.'

'Oh yeah?!' Serendipity sneered. 'How do you do that then? Wave a magic wand?!' With this image in mind, Serendipity couldn't help but laugh at the thought of the parrot waving a wand.

Yet, Pollyanna just smiled and said, 'Well, I suppose I do create a certain sort of magic – although there is no wand! The magic comes from inside *you* Serendipity. I'm really just a sort of guide, helping you find it. It's then up to you how you use it!'

'Magic inside me? What a load of tosh,' Serendipity spat. 'Anyway, if there's magic inside me, why don't you just *tell* me exactly where to find it instead of getting me to play hide and seek!?'

'That wouldn't work as well,' replied Polly patiently. 'You see, as a wise person once said, *'Knowledge of what is, does not open the door directly to what should be.'*[3]

Serendipity was perplexed by this statement. 'What on earth does that mean?' she asked, rolling her eyes with exasperation.

Polly just smiled patiently and replied, 'Discovering what it means is the final step to finding the magic. When you discover the magic you are close to realising your dreams.'

---

[3] Albert Einstein (1879–1955).

11

Serendipity was unconvinced by what the parrot was saying, so replied sarcastically, 'So if I had a dream then you could make that come true – with a bunch of riddles and no magic wand? *Yeah right!*'

'I could indeed,' Polly replied, 'but you have to want something enough and trust me to be your guide.'

'How do I trust you when I don't even know you?!' scoffed Serendipity. Yet, although highly suspicious of such a claim, she was also intrigued by what the parrot was saying.

Seemingly unfazed by Serendipity's resistance, Polly continued, 'To discover the magic, you really do need to trust me. Think of me as being your most loyal friend, someone who will put your needs first, who will be there for you no matter what, who will support you when the going gets tough and never give up on you, even when you feel like giving up on yourself.'

Serendipity laughed out loud. 'I don't need any friends and I certainly don't need anyone else's help – especially not from some strange parrot I've only just met! Besides why would you help me when you don't even know me?'

Pollyanna sighed. 'Oh, but I don't need to *know* you Serendipity. All I need to know is that you have a dream – and I am here to help make it come true. However, if you don't want my help, I guess that's your choice. After all, I can only help those who *do* want my help. You won't find the magic unless you actually go *looking* for it and trust me to be your guide.'

As Serendipity listened to what Pollyanna was saying she realised that, however much she hated to admit it, she *could* do with a friend in her life right now. Besides, however much she resisted, the parrot's talk of dreams and magic made her curious to find out more.

'So, if you're some sort of dream-maker, what are you doing in my house?' Serendipity asked, trying not to sound *too* interested in the answer.

'You just got lucky I guess,' sighed Polly. 'You see, I have spent my life travelling around the world helping others, just like you. Once I have helped them to achieve their dreams, I move on to help someone else. I just hop out of my cage and make my way to another pet store and wait for someone else to buy me.'

As Pollyanna talked, Serendipity became more and more intrigued by the parrot and her strange stories. So intrigued, in fact, that she could feel her guard slowly starting to slip.

'So,' she asked, allowing herself to sound a little more curious this time, 'who exactly have you helped then?'

Polly ruffled her feathers. 'Oh, all sorts. Anyone who wants my help really. You see, *everyone* has dreams, Serendipity. Everyone has something about their life that they would like to change, even *you*, I'm sure!'

Listening to what Pollyanna was saying, Serendipity began to acknowledge that maybe, just maybe, the parrot did have a point. This thought forced her to squirm a little uncomfortably. She then asked tentatively, 'So what, er, sort of things do they wish for then?'

Pollyanna smiled warmly. 'Oh, all sorts of things. Let's see ... things such as a more fulfilling career, some new hobbies, a better relationship ... or even a *new* relationship, a better balance of work and family life, better parenting skills, a healthier lifestyle, more confidence, more excitement, more freedom, less stress ... The list goes on and on.'

As Pollyanna talked, Serendipity thought about this list and how wonderful it all sounded. However, she really had no desire to admit this to a parrot she hardly knew!

So, not wanting to expose such vulnerability, she said casually but defiantly, 'Well, I really don't need your help as I'm happy with my life as it is, thank you very much!'

Despite Serendipity's abrupt response, Pollyanna just said, 'Well then, that's up to you. However, there are plenty of others out there who *do* want my help, so I guess I will soon be moving on then.'

With those words, Serendipity was suddenly struck with the

realisation that, despite her initial resistance to the parrot's offer of help, she didn't *really* want Polly to go.

So, not wanting to admit this to the bird, she merely replied, 'I guess you will then. I'm just *not* the sort of cat who believes in magic. I sort out my own problems, thank you very much. That sort of stuff is for sissies anyway!'

As she said these words, Serendipity tossed her head back with such defiance it set off a headache she knew would probably be with her for the rest of day.

With that final exchange, the cat and the bird sat where they were, neither saying a word, Serendipity's head throbbing with pain and Pollyanna's feathers gently blowing in the breeze which was now coming in from the open window.

After what seemed like an eternity, it was Serendipity who finally broke the silence. 'Right, I'm off then!' she announced, with an air of determination.

'OK then, nice meeting you,' replied Polly, still unfazed by the cat's petulance.

'Right then,' said Serendipity, turning her back on the parrot.

Yet, as she began to walk away, she couldn't help but wonder more about Pollyanna and her story of dreams and magic. She thought back to the list of wishes Polly had said others often had. Were there *really* so many others out there who wanted so much to change their lives?

She found this hard to believe when she looked out of the window at the other cats in the lane. From where she was sitting, it seemed like everyone else led a truly charmed life filled with fun and happiness. Yet, was that really true and, if she was honest, how great was her own life when she really thought about it?

She considered her daily routine of lying in her basket, catching a few mice, eating, drinking and watching the world go by. When she thought about the hours she spent looking out of the conservatory window, she had to ask herself – *was she in fact just an observer rather than a participant in life?*

It then occurred to Serendipity that Polly had so far raised far more questions than she had provided answers. As a result, Serendipity was now becoming increasingly curious to find out more about the parrot, where she had come from and why she had arrived at her house that day. She even began to wonder if perhaps she should tell Pollyanna about the Dairy and the Cream of Life.

As the minutes passed and her mind again turned to thoughts of cream, she considered that maybe, just maybe, she should give the parrot a chance to help. After all, what was there really to lose?

So, feeling a little embarrassed but now determined to find some answers, Serendipity slowly turned back towards the study.

Leaving her pride at the door, she once again came face to face with Pollyanna.

3

'*True happiness can be sought, thought or caught – but never bought*' [4]

Serendipity stood in front of the parrot's cage. Despite her considerable nerves she cleared her throat, cocked her head nonchalantly to one side and, trying her hardest to sound casual, began to talk.

'Er ... Pollyanna ... I ... I've been thinking.'

Polly looked up and smiled. 'Yes, I'm listening. And please, do call me Polly.'

'Well, in that case,' replied Serendipity, feeling her guard slowly slipping, 'then maybe you should shorten my name too. Serendipity is such a mouthful!'

Polly gently shook her head. 'Why shorten it?' she replied, 'Serendipity is such a beautiful name – it suits you down to the ground!'

Serendipity could feel herself blushing underneath her fur. 'I'm not sure I like it, my owners gave it to me when I moved in two years ago.'

'Do you know what it means?'

'Well, actually no. Does it mean something?'

'You will find out in good time,' replied Polly with a wink. 'When the time is right, it will become clear to you exactly what your name means and why it was given to you!'

Serendipity was perplexed by what the parrot was saying.

---

[4] Anonymous.

17

However, not really sure how to respond to this revelation, she merely replied with a laugh, 'Well, in that case, maybe I should hang around to find out.'

'Maybe indeed you should!' laughed Polly.

As Serendipity began to laugh with Polly, she could feel herself slowly warming to this mysterious parrot. And, for the first time in a long, long while, she felt comfortable talking to someone else about herself.

'So, what was it you wanted to tell me?' asked Polly when they had finished laughing.

'Well,' replied Serendipity, 'what I wanted to say was ... I guess I do have a *sort* of dream.'

'Great, well, tell me more!' Polly said with encouragement.

'Well, I've never really told anyone before ... and, well, you would probably just laugh if I told you.'

'Try me,' Pollyanna replied warmly.

So, taking a deep breath, Serendipity began to tell the parrot about the farm with a dairy far, far away, where cats could drink as much cream as they wanted and all their dreams would come true, and the parrot listened.

When Serendipity had finally finished her story, Polly blew a long, low whistle through her beak and said, 'That sounds wonderful, Serendipity! However, please tell me – *what would you wish for if you reached the Dairy and got to drink the Cream of Life?*'

What a daft question! thought Serendipity. *The answer was obvious wasn't it?*

'Well, I would wish that all my dreams would come true!' she said, rolling her eyes.

'OK,' replied Polly patiently. 'But Serendipity, what *are* your dreams?'

As Serendipity opened her mouth to speak, to her utter surprise nothing came out.

Hard as she tried, she couldn't think of an answer to this particular question.

As she struggled to think of a good dream to have, it occurred to her that she had never really given it that much thought before. She had always imagined that just drinking the Cream of Life would be enough to solve all her problems and make her happy. Yet, now she was forced to think about what her dreams actually were, the more she tried to think of an answer, the more her mind went blank.

'Well ... I ... I don't know,' she eventually stammered. 'I guess I never really thought about it that much before because, well, deep down I suppose I never really believed the Cream actually existed!'

'But Serendipity, if you don't have dreams, then how can you have your dreams come true?' the parrot enquired patiently.

As Serendipity listened to what Polly had to say, she realised that the parrot was indeed right. Now she thought about it, she was fairly sure that she *used* to have hopes and dreams.

She was not sure at what point *exactly* she had given up dreaming, but she guessed it might have been around the time she had been given her *comfortable warm basket*.

Polly could see Serendipity was struggling to answer this particular question, so began by asking, 'So, if you *did* know what your dream was, what would you wish for?'

'If I *did* know?' replied Serendipity hesitantly. Yet, as she asked herself this question, as if by magic, she began to feel clearer about what might be a good dream to have.

'Well ... er, I guess I would wish that I could win the cat lotto and live in a big house, with lots of nice food, an even bigger basket and never have to do any work again – especially not boring, tedious mousing!'

Polly nodded patiently. 'OK, and why do you want to have those things?'

ANOTHER dumb question, thought Serendipity.
After all, who wouldn't want to have them?!
EVERYONE WANTED THEM.
They were good things to have – WEREN'T THEY?!

Yet, despite her irritation with this question, Serendipity tried her best to provide an answer for Polly.

So, she opened her mouth to speak. 'Well ... er, they would make me ... well, I would be ... er, *happy* I guess.'

Serendipity realised this wasn't the clear, concise answer she had hoped to give Polly. However, it was the only answer she could think of right at that moment.

She looked over to see Polly's reaction. But the parrot just nodded and said, 'Tell me Serendipity, what does the word *happiness* mean to you?'

Gosh that's another dumb question to add to the list, thought Serendipity, and without hesitation replied, 'Well, that's obvious! It means, er ... well, I suppose ... well ... not being *sad* I guess!'

'OK, but that's focusing on what you *don't* want to feel,' said Polly patiently. 'However, we only want to focus on what you *do* want to feel. So, let's try again with a positive definition!'

On reflection, Serendipity could see that Polly did have a point. *Not being sad* was an unsatisfactory definition of being happy!

So, taking Polly's advice, Serendipity took a deep breath and tried again.

'Well, happiness would mean I was ... happy ... felt very happy ... um ... good ... and ... erm ... happy!'

As Serendipity once more struggled to answer this question, it occurred to her that she had never really stopped to think about what it meant to be happy. She had always assumed that she *should* be happy if she had her basket, her food and a roof over her head. She also assumed she would be *even happier* if she had an even bigger basket, more food, a bigger house to live in and never have to work again. But after talking to Polly, for the first time in her life, it occurred to her that maybe she was confusing the word 'happy' with the word 'comfortable'.

Seeing Serendipity struggle with her definition of happiness, Polly intervened. 'Serendipity, let's try something else. I want you to think back to a time in your life when you felt the most happy. As you think back I want you to relax and let your mind run free. Tell me everything about the experience. Tell me all about what you were doing and what you were feeling. Make sure you use all your senses to make the description as detailed as possible.'

Serendipity immediately thought what a hard task that was. When did she last feel truly happy? She certainly couldn't remember a time recently. Yet, determined to provide a decent answer this time, she took Polly's advice and let her mind relax. As she did so, she felt herself slowly drifting back in time to when she was a kitten.

At this point, she took in another deep breath and began.

'Well, when I was a kitten I *think* I felt happy.' Not quite sure if this was the correct reply, Serendipity paused and looked at Polly for reassurance.

Polly just nodded and said encouragingly, 'Yes, Serendipity, tell me all about when you were a kitten.'

Serendipity took another breath and continued.

'Well, I remember being around my brothers and sisters and we were having lots of fun.'

Again Serendipity paused and looked at Polly for reassurance.

'And what were you doing that was fun?' Polly asked warmly.

Serendipity tried to remember what she used to do as a kitten. 'Well, I remember running around playing chase the ball. I remember it was good sharing things and having others around to talk to and play with.'

Polly nodded and said, 'So, how did this make you feel?'

Serendipity struggled to think back to how she had felt. As the images became more vivid, she was aware of becoming more and more connected with how she had felt at the time.

'Well, I suppose when I think back to when I was a kitten, what I remember feeling most was *excitement*. I particularly

21

remember that I really looked forward to each new day. Every day was different, with lots of fun things to do. I loved the freedom of running around and making friends with the other cats who lived nearby. We would have such adventures together! I would always go to bed excited, wondering what we would do the next day.

'I also loved knowing that I really belonged to a family. We all got on so well and lived in blissful harmony. When the day was done, I enjoyed snuggling up to my mum at night and I felt really loved. Yes, it was feeling *loved* that I remember most clearly.'

Serendipity paused and once again looked up at Polly.

But Polly just nodded and said, 'That's great Serendipity, tell me more about how you felt.'

Serendipity took another deep breath. The more she thought back to her childhood, the clearer the images became and the stronger the feelings associated with them grew.

'Well, I particularly remember how exciting it was when we first got to go outside and my mum took us mouse hunting. I wasn't that good at it to start with, but I enjoyed it anyway. My brothers and sisters would all compete with me so it was a bit of a challenge! Although it was hard work, I thought it was fun having a go and, when I improved, I felt so proud of what I had achieved. I particularly loved teaching the other kittens what I had learned. I enjoyed this responsibility and feeling of independence. I suppose I felt I had a role to play, a sense of purpose and valued the respect I earned from others. I didn't agree with killing other animals so I taught the other cats it was good to let the mice go. I felt so proud that they had learned this from me.'

As Serendipity recalled her childhood memories, the feelings of excitement and pride grew stronger with each passing word. When she had finished talking, she sighed and said, 'Those were the best days of my life.'

Polly listened intently to what Serendipity was saying, nodding with encouragement as she spoke.

Polly then asked, 'So, from what you have just said, would I be correct in concluding that fun, excitement, challenges, a sense of achievement, a sense of purpose, responsibility, freedom, independence, variety, feeling proud, feeling respected, family, love, helping others and sharing are high on your list of values?'

Serendipity was confused. 'What, er, what do you mean by *values*?'

Polly nodded patiently and began to explain. 'A value is something that is personal to you, that reflects who you are and what is important to you. In simple terms they are what you should be getting up for in the morning! They can be principles you live by and qualities you value in yourself, others and the world around you. Honouring the values in your life is an important step to finding happiness.'

Serendipity wasn't sure she totally understood this explanation. So, to gain clarification she asked cautiously, 'So, the times when I felt most happy in my life were the times when I was most honouring my own values?'

Polly nodded in agreement. 'Exactly, and lack of contentment is most likely to occur when those values are *not* being honoured. If you pursue a dream that doesn't honour your own values, you are unlikely to achieve that dream and, even if you do, you are unlikely to find true happiness from achieving it.'

Serendipity considered what Polly had just revealed about values.

'So, that's why I couldn't come up with a reason *why* I wanted a big house, a big basket and never having to work again – because by pursuing and achieving those things I wouldn't have been honouring my values?'

Polly replied with a knowing look, 'Well, if your values include fun, excitement, a sense of purpose, challenge, feeling proud, variety, love, helping others and sharing, then I guess you have your answer!'

When Serendipity thought about what Polly had just said, the principle of values suddenly became crystal clear. In that moment, she realised she was not currently honouring her values at all and this went a long way to explaining why she felt so unfulfilled with her life as it was.

'Right,' said Polly, ruffling her tail feathers. 'What I want you to do now is to take a trip into the future. I want you to close your eyes and imagine you are an old cat of, say, about twenty! I want you to tell me about your life and everything that you have achieved. Tell me all about what has happened to you and is still happening. Tell me about all the things you have done, how you felt and why they were important to you.'

'Gosh,' said Serendipity excitedly. 'First I looked into the past and now I have to go into the future – what an adventure! I feel like a time traveller from one of those movies!'

So, with a feeling of anticipation and excitement, she once again let her mind relax and an image of an imaginary future began slowly to form.

When the image was clear she began to tell Polly the story of her life.

'Well, many, many years ago I found the courage to leave my comfortable warm basket and make the long and perilous journey to the Celestial Dairy.'

Serendipity paused, not quite sure what to say next.

'Yes, what happened next?' asked Polly reassuringly.

As Serendipity began to relax, some more images of her future life began to form.

'Well,' she said, 'I was scared at first, but, when I had taken that first step, I felt so proud. I had many adventures on the way to the Dairy and, when I eventually arrived there, I got to drink as much cream as I liked. When I drank the Cream of Life, all my dreams came true. I had many happy years living at the Dairy. Living there gave me a real sense of belonging and

I felt part of a happy community. I lived a life full of fun and excitement and made many friends. I soon met a gorgeous tom who shared my dreams and my values. We had many adventures together over the years and eventually we had a family of our own. I felt lots of love for my family and enjoyed watching my kittens grow into adults. I enjoyed teaching them all about life and how to be successful and happy. I was really proud to see them develop their personalities and own set of values. I felt so happy myself because I had a real sense of purpose, with each new day presenting me with a new challenge and adventure.'

When Serendipity had finished, Polly let out a loud whistle through her beak. 'Wow, Serendipity! That's an amazing life you've led! Now tell me this – how do you feel when you look back over this long and happy life?'

Serendipity smiled. 'Yes, it was indeed a long and happy life. In fact, I look back over my life with a real sense of achievement and pride.'

'That's fantastic!' exclaimed Polly. 'We will now go even further into the future. You have indeed lived a long and happy life. You are now about to meet your maker and depart to the big cattery in the sky. Someone close to you is about to make a speech at your funeral and its all about *you*. I want you now to tell me exactly what you would want them to say in that speech.'

Serendipity was stunned. 'Gosh, my *funeral*?! That's a hard one! I've never really thought about death before.'

Yet, now she was forced to think about her own mortality, it brought home to her how important it was to make sure she lived her life to the fullest.

So, with that in mind, Serendipity began to think about what she would like others to say about her when she was dead.

At first her mind went blank. Yet, determined not to give up, she tried to relax and to let her mind run free as she had done before.

25

When she could feel the ideas beginning to flow, she took a deep breath and began.

'Today we say goodbye to Serendipity, the most wonderful friend a cat could ever have.' Hesitating, she looked over towards Polly for reassurance.

Polly simply nodded and said, 'Yes, Serendipity, go on ... '

So, Serendipity took another deep breath and continued. 'I say this because you could always rely on her loyalty and support whenever times were tough. Serendipity was someone you knew you could always trust and you knew she would always be there for you no matter what.'

As Serendipity talked, she was aware of the ideas and words now beginning to freely flow. So, she continued with increasing confidence.

'You always knew that just being around Serendipity would make you feel good, even when you were feeling down. Her sense of fun was infectious and she was always such wonderful company. You certainly knew there would never be a dull moment when Serendipity was around! She never let a problem get her down and made sure she went after her dreams no matter what! She was kind, generous and, above all, always happy. She was definitely an inspiration to others. She will be sorely missed.'

When Serendipity had finished talking she was stunned at what she had just said about herself.

She looked up at Polly who was clapping her wings with great enthusiasm.

'Well done, Serendipity! That's fantastic! Now, after hearing that speech, am I right in thinking we can add friendship, loyalty, trust, positivity and integrity to your list of values?'

'Yes, yes, you can!' replied Serendipity excitedly. 'Now I think about it, I realise they are very important to me indeed!'

Yet, as Serendipity considered what she had just said about the person she would like to be and the excitement she had felt when she had said it, she was also aware of a heaviness overwhelming her. In that moment, her eyes started to well up with tears.

'What's wrong Serendipity?' the parrot enquired with concern.

Serendipity gulped, feeling a lump beginning to form in her throat.

'Well, you see,' she explained, 'although I feel good about all the things I have just said, I also feel sad.'

'What do you feel sad about?'

'I feel sad because currently I'm not honouring my values at all. When I talk about how I would like my life to be, it brings home to me just how meaningless it is at the moment. As for my funeral speech, if I died right now I don't think anyone would even notice that I was gone, let alone say such wonderful things about me.' As she spoke, Serendipity wiped a tear from the corner of her eye.

'Well, that's actually a positive thing!' Polly said with encouragement.

'How can it possibly be a positive thing?' Serendipity replied, dabbing her eyes.

'Well, can you remember what you said to me when I first offered you my help?'

As Serendipity thought back to when she had first met Polly and recalled the negative reception she had initially given her, she was overcome with embarrassment and replied in no more than a whisper, 'I said I was fine, I didn't need any friends and I didn't need your help.'

Polly merely nodded and said, 'Yes, indeed you did; and how do you feel about my help now?'

Serendipity hung her head, not wanting to meet Polly's gaze. 'I feel grateful and relieved as I have now admitted that things are not so fine and I would indeed love for things to be different. Well ... not just different but much, much better!'

Polly nodded in agreement. 'Well done, Serendipity, that is

an important first step because *you can't change what you don't acknowledge.*'

As Serendipity pondered this statement, it slowly dawned on her that she had in fact been living in denial for quite some time.

'I suppose it was so much easier to be in denial than face up to the truth that my life is ... well ... not that great after all,' she finally said, overcome with a mixture of embarrassment and relief.

'Well, as they say, "better late than never", and remember, it's never too late to begin to make changes in your life! As a wise person once said, "*It's never too late to be what you might have been*".'[5]

'I do hope not,' replied Serendipity tentatively.

'Don't just hope – believe!' exclaimed Polly encouragingly. 'But what we need to do now is to think about what each section of your life would look like in detail if you got to drink the Cream of Life.'

'What sections are you talking about?' enquired Serendipity, scratching behind her ear.

'Well,' replied Polly, 'how about breaking your life down into the following areas: physical environment; social life; family life; love life; physical well-being; emotional and spiritual well-being; career; recreation; financial situation; and any other area you feel is important to you. You will need to have a detailed idea of how you would like each section of your life to be if you got to drink the Cream. You can then compare this with how things are at the moment.'

'Wow!' exclaimed Serendipity, wiping her brow. 'That sounds like a mighty big task to me!'

'I quite understand,' replied Polly sympathetically. 'It may well take some time for you to do this. How about you have a

---

[5] George Eliot (English writer, 1819–1880).

go at this task on your own and then come back to see me when you've finished.'

'But I don't know when I can next come back to see you,' said Serendipity, suddenly filled with anxiety. 'My owners are normally hanging around, so they might wonder what I'm doing in here!'

'So, what are they doing right now?' enquired Polly.

Serendipity stopped to think for a moment. 'I assume they must be shopping as they normally go out this time each week and come back with lots of bags. This is the only time I know for sure they will be gone. I don't think I'll be able to come back and see you again until this time next week.'

'Not to worry,' said Polly reassuringly. 'That will give you plenty of time to think through what we've talked about today. When it's time to come back next week, I will keep a lookout and then whistle to let you know that the coast is clear!'

At that moment, they heard a door slam and Serendipity knew that her owners must be back from their shopping trip.

'I'd better get back to my basket or they'll know something's up,' Serendipity explained, her heart thumping loudly in her chest.

'Well, good luck,' said Polly, ruffling her feathers. 'It's been great talking to you!'

Serendipity turned and waved her paw. 'Thanks Polly, I'll get on with the task you've set straight away! See you the same time next week!'

She then ran as quickly as she could back to her seat in the window.

As she settled back down into her basket, she was once again faced with the familiar view out of the window. She saw the garden below, leading to the fields beyond and the smoke that was still rising from behind the furthest hill.

Although it was basically the same view she had seen earlier that morning, somehow it now looked slightly different. The flowers in the garden seemed somewhat brighter, the field

29

somewhat greener, the sun somewhat stronger and the smoke somehow nearer.

Serendipity could also see that the sun had now sunk lower in the sky. It was then that she realised how long she must have been talking to Polly. Yet, how quickly the time had gone! Polly had given her so much to think about that it felt like the thoughts were literally flooding her mind!

She looked over at her bowl and saw that it was still empty. Yet, Serendipity really didn't mind as she now had other things to think about besides her next meal.

As she settled down into her basket to begin the task Polly had set her, she began to notice a nagging feeling in the pit of her stomach – and she was sure it wasn't hunger! *What would Polly think if she couldn't do the task and couldn't come up with the answers?* she wondered. Yet, despite these worries, she was determined to give it a try. After all, she had already developed a feeling of loyalty to the parrot even though they had only just met that day. She really couldn't let Polly down now! Not only that, she realised she couldn't let *herself* down now that she had a taste of what it was like to dream.

She realised that she wouldn't be able to relax until she had something worthy to bring back to Polly the next week.

As Serendipity sat in her basket and looked out of the window, she reflected on what a strange day she had just had. In fact, she had to admit it was probably the strangest day of her life.

Who would have thought the day would have turned out this way?

She recalled how she had woken up that morning filled with apathy for the usual routine that lay ahead. Yet now she had met a strange parrot, made a new friend and had dared to dream about a new life. Yet, there were a couple of things that Polly had said which still perplexed her.

'Knowledge of what is, does not open the door directly to what should be.'

She recalled how Polly had said that finding the answer to this riddle would be the final step towards realising her dreams. Yet at this point she had no idea what it could possibly mean.

Polly had also said she would discover the meaning of her name when the time was right.

As the sense of fatigue overwhelmed her, she realised that perhaps now was not the time to try to work out these particular riddles. As she settled deeper into her basket, she decided to reflect on what she had learned from Polly that day:

* Face up to denial. You can't change what you don't acknowledge!
* Dare to dream. If you don't have a dream then you can't have a dream come true.
* Having to face her immortality, she realised it was important to lead a life she could be proud of and one that made her happy.
* She now had a clearer idea of what it meant to be happy.
* She was most happy when she was honouring her values.
* Her values were what she should be getting up for in the morning.
* Her values consisted of qualities and principles she valued in her life, herself and others.

What she valued in her life

* A challenge
* A sense of purpose
* A sense of achievement
* A sense of responsibility
* A sense of community
* A sense of belonging
* Independence

- Excitement
- Fun
- Family
- Harmony
- Helping others
- Sharing with others
- Feeling loved
- Freedom of choice
- Variety

What she valued in herself and others

- Generosity
- Kindness
- Friendship
- Loyalty
- Trust
- Integrity
- Positivity
- Respect
- Working hard

She now needed to have a clearer idea about what her life would look like if she got to drink the Cream. She knew she had a week to complete this task, so wanted to do it to the best of her ability.

She once again looked out of the window and saw that the sun was beginning to set behind the clouds that had now formed in the sky. It wouldn't be long before daylight turned to darkness.

Finally succumbing to exhaustion, she was aware of her eyes beginning to close. *Time for bed* she thought, and snuggled once more into the comfort of her basket. Yet, despite her exhaustion, that night Serendipity found it hard to sleep.

For the first time in two years, her basket didn't feel quite so comfortable any more.

Was it because it was now slightly too small for her – or had she finally grown too big for it?

Throughout the night she tossed and turned, trying hard to get comfortable. Yet, the more she tried to get comfortable, the more out of place she felt lying there in her basket.

When she finally drifted off to sleep, she dreamed of cream and her new life at the Celestial Dairy.

4

'If dreams were for sale, what would you buy?'[6]

W hen Serendipity finally awoke, she was aware of a stiffness and aching in her limbs. This was indeed an unusual feeling first thing in the morning!

She then remembered the dream she had had the night before and immediately forgot about the aches and pains. Instead, she considered the task that lay ahead. This task was to have a detailed idea of what her life would be like if she got to drink the Cream.

But how would she go about doing this?

She then recalled how Polly had mentioned the need to divide her life up into sections. After much thought, she decided the best way to do this was to draw a circle which would represent her life. The circle could then be divided up into the required sections.

But, what should she include in each section?

After a little thought she remembered what Polly had suggested. These sections were physical environment, social life, love life, family life, career, financial situation, recreation, physical well-being and emotional well-being.

As she went through this list, she began to feel a little overwhelmed.

Was there really this much to the average life?!

---

[6] Thomas Beddoes (physician/philosopher, 1760–1808).

Not wishing to give up so soon, she found a piece of paper, drew a circle and divided it up into sections. As she studied the circle, she considered how it looked just like a wheel, with spokes running from the centre. Feeling suddenly inspired by what she had drawn, she thought to herself, *I will call this my Wheel of Life!*

At first she felt unsure about where to start, realising that she had never really thought to break down her life in this way before. Without Polly to guide her, she had to admit to feeling a little lost. Yet, she knew how important it was that she complete the task before she saw the parrot again.

With this in mind, she immediately began to work on the first section of her Wheel of Life:

Area 1 – Physical Environment

So, if she got to drink the cream, where would she like to live?

Well, firstly, she would like to live in a nice big house with plenty of room to run around. An equally big garden would be good too. A warm basket was essential and preferably one with lots of room! A decent view too. Maybe even a view of the sea! A cosy warm fire would be good as well – one she could cuddle up to on a cold winter's night! She would also need regular meals with plenty of variety. Lots of lovely cream to drink too of course!

She considered how good this all sounded. Yes, it sounded very good indeed!

Yet, why did she want these things?

She immediately recalled what Polly had said about honouring her values. So, if she had these things, would she be honouring her values by acquiring them?

On the face of it, much to her disappointment, she couldn't really see how any of her values would be honoured by filling up this section of her Wheel.

So, on a scale of 1–10 of importance to her overall happiness, filling up this section would probably only be about 1.

So what was her physical environment like right now?

Well, she did have a nice house to live in (although not a particularly big one), a pretty garden (although she never went in it), a comfy warm basket (although it did seem a bit small now), regular meals (although the same boring tuna every day) and a decent view (although not of the sea!). Yet, she *didn't* have a cosy warm fire in the winter – and she was definitely lacking in the cream department!

However, overall, her present physical environment was pretty good, if a little restricted.

Points out of 10? Probably about 7.

Overall gap between dream and reality? Probably not that big!

This is a good start! Serendipity thought with a smile. Maybe this task wouldn't be so hard after all.

She looked out of the window and saw a big grey cat saunter by and then disappear into one of the larger houses next door. She instantly thought how lucky the cat was to have such a big house to live in. She considered that if the house was so big, it probably had an enormous garden to run around in too!

As she looked at the smoke pouring from the house's chimney, she realised it must also have a lovely warm fire to snuggle up to.

With all these thoughts flooding through her mind, Serendipity suddenly didn't feel quite so good about where she was living right now. In fact, she felt very dissatisfied indeed!

However, thinking back once more to her set of values, she was reminded that the importance of filling this particular section was probably not a priority if she was to achieve true happiness.

So, to summarise:
Current situation: 7 out of 10

37

Importance to overall happiness: 1 out of 10
Priority of filling this section: Low

Area 2 – Social Life

So, if she got to drink the Cream, how would she like her social life to be?

She immediately thought back to when she was a kitten and remembered how good it felt to have other cats to play with. So, if she got to drink the Cream, she would like to have lots of cats to talk to and share some adventures with! Yes, fun and adventures were definitely important to her! Yet, it would be good to have at least *one* special friend.

Since meeting Polly she had realised how nice it was to have someone you could talk to and who really cared about you. Yes, she now realised how sharing was important, particularly sharing thoughts and feelings.

She thought back to her values and realised that filling this section was very important to her. In fact, probably about 8 out of 10.

So, where was she now?

Well, she had no friends at all, not even one special friend. Neither did she ever go out and have fun. However, she *did* concede that she was at least now able to talk to Polly about her feelings.

Yet, despite this fact, she still had to face the reality that it was definitely looking like a low score for this section.

Maybe 1 out of 10 if she was being generous!

To her dismay, she considered what a mighty big gap there appeared to be between dream and reality in this section of the Wheel!

Feeling a little down, she once again looked out of the window. Her eyes were immediately drawn to the sight of Ginger and Tabby chasing after a ball. Being a natural athlete, Tabby seemed to be at a distinct advantage, leaving Ginger trailing behind. Yet, Ginger still appeared to have a lot of fun trying to keep up!

Looking at the scene unfolding before her, Serendipity was suddenly struck by a feeling of loneliness and isolation as she sat there all alone in her basket.

She reflected on how important this section was to honouring her values and how empty it presently was.

To summarise:
Current situation: 1 out of 10
Importance to overall happiness: 8 out of 10
Priority of filling this section: High

Maybe she would do better on the next section of her Wheel of Life.

But what was the next section?

When Serendipity realised what came next, she felt a lump begin to form in her throat.

Area 3 – Love Life

With a sense of foreboding, Serendipity realised this was going to be even harder than the previous sections. Having to imagine something she had never experienced before was indeed going to be a challenge! However, despite this fact, she was determined to at least give it a try.

So, if she got to drink the Cream of Life, how would she like this section to look?

Well, firstly, she would like to be in love with a kind and thoughtful tom. They would have lots of fun together and go out on many adventures. They would spend romantic nights under the stars and share their hopes and dreams over dinners of fine food and cream. Yes, they would *definitely* share lots of cream! He would then ask her to marry him and they would live happily ever after with their fine litter of kittens! Serendipity couldn't help but smile as she thought about how wonderful this would be!

But her smile soon disappeared when she realised that in reality the score for this section was a resounding 0.

Yes, this section of the Wheel was definitely looking very empty indeed!

So why did she want these things? She again thought back to her list of values. She was immediately reminded of how important family, sharing, and giving and receiving love were to her. She then realised how important this section of her Wheel of Life was to achieving happiness. In fact, probably about 8 out of 10.

To summarise:
Current situation: 0
Importance to overall happiness: 8 out of 10
Priority of filling this section: High

To her dismay she realised this was another section with a high score for importance yet a low score for reality.

As she looked out of the window, she was greeted with the sight of Smudge and Spot snuggled up together under their favourite rhododendron bush. She considered how wonderful it must be to be that much in love. She then felt a small tear forming in the corner of her eye as she was once again over-whelmed by a sense of emptiness.

Better get on to the next section, she thought, as she wiped away the tear with her paw.

Area 4 – Family Life

Right, I think at least I can score a few points here! she thought, feeling a little more positive.

So, if she got to drink the Cream, how would she like her family life to be?

Well, for a start, she would like to have a loving family who gave her lots of attention and cuddles. It would also be good to sit on someone's lap and have her coat stroked while watching some TV! Yes, it would definitely be good to feel really valued as a member of the household. It would also be wonderful to have a family of her own with plenty of time to spend with them all. She would also dearly love to see her parents again and spend some quality time with her siblings.

So, why did she want these things? Thinking once more about her set of values, she realised that this was another very important section of her Wheel of Life. In fact, she would say it scored 9 out of 10 for importance.

As she thought about her own cat family, her mind went back to how she had been adopted at three months old by her present human family, comprising of mother, father and a little girl. She remembered how her new human family had changed her name and then taken her away from her brothers and sisters. She recalled how at first she had received lots of attention, especially from the little girl. Yet, as she had grown older, the family seemed to lose interest in her. She remembered how rejected she had then felt and how, over time, she had gone out less and less, finally withdrawing into the comfort of her basket.

Serendipity paused, wiping another tear from her eye.

When she had managed to compose herself she continued with the task.

So, where was she right now?

As she thought about what her home life was currently like, she realised to her dismay that she wouldn't be able to score many points here either.

41

Well, maybe scrape together one or two if she was lucky!

However, she conceded that she did at least belong to a family who looked after her and generally made sure she was fed and watered – which was good. Some cats didn't have a family at all, so in some ways she was luckier than others.

Yet, despite all this, she realised that she felt no more valued than a piece of old furniture. Her family never really acknowledged her presence, and certainly never invited her into the living room to watch TV. She was definitely never greeted with a hug or ever stroked. In fact, she didn't think anyone would even notice if she went missing! When it came down to it, she felt she was *tolerated* rather than loved.

And, as for her own cat family, she didn't even know where her parents were now, let alone her brothers and sisters. So, the total score for this section was probably no more than 2.

To summarise:
Current situation: 2 out of 10
Importance for overall happiness: 9 out of 10
Priority of filling this section: High

As she looked out of the window, she saw a little boy come out from one of the houses in the lane and sweep Tabby up in his arms. He then gave the cat a big hug.

Better move on to another section, Serendipity thought, feeling a lump beginning to form in her throat.

Area 5 – Career

So, if she got to drink the cream, what career would she like to have?

As she tried to think about what career she would like, Serendipity soon realised that she wasn't *at all* sure what she would like to do. She had never really thought about changing jobs before, just accepting that her present job as a mouser was the only job she could or would ever do.

After all, her parents were both mousers and she thought that her brothers and sisters probably were too. She had never really bothered to explore what other options might be available to a cat such as herself.

However, now she was forced to think about what she would really like to do with her life, she felt herself struggling for ideas.

She began to recall what she had said to Polly about her ideal life and the values that she held dear. As she did so, a picture of her ideal job began to slowly form in her mind.

Firstly, her ideal job would need to be fun and rewarding – and *well rewarded*! However, she wasn't exactly sure at this point what job would be fun and rewarding.

Yet, she felt sure that 'fun and rewarding' was important!

So, where was she now?

Present job: mouser.

Fun and rewarding? Definitely not.

In fact, she had to admit to being bored out of her mind. For a start, there didn't appear to be many mice to catch anyway. Yet, despite this fact, she would still go about her usual routine of getting up late, having a quick look round the house, see there were no mice around and then go back to her basket. In fact, some days she didn't even bother to get out of her basket at all! Besides, as she had explained to Polly, she didn't really like killing mice as it went against her principles.

She also recalled from her list of values how important it was to have a challenge, to share and to help others. She remembered how excitement and variety had also been important to her when she was a kitten.

Thinking about her set of values, she now realised how important filling this section was to her overall happiness. In fact, she would say it was about 9 out of 10.

When she thought again about her job as a mouser, she

considered how there was presently no challenge at all to her work, no sense of variety, no sharing and definitely no sense of helping others. She certainly wasn't helping her owners very much anyway!

This exercise had made her realise that her present job was definitely *not* in line with her core values and this probably explained why she wasn't much good at freeing the house of mice! Consequently, she was *not* well rewarded. In fact, quite often the opposite!

'Hopeless' and 'useless' were the words she often heard muttered from her owners' lips. Now she thought about it, those were the only times her presence was ever really acknowledged!

Maybe that was why she only got tuna to eat!

So, what was her overall score on this section?

On reflection, probably only 1 for effort.

To summarise:
Current situation: 1 out of 10
Importance for overall happiness: 9 out of 10
Priority for filling this section: Very high

Yet another section which scored high on importance yet low on reality!

Feeling a little down about this score, she looked out the window once more for inspiration. Out of the corner of her eye she spied Ginger spitting aggressively, seeing off another cat as it unwittingly approached his driveway. She knew from studying Ginger's behaviour that he was a guard cat. Serendipity reflected on how she had often admired Ginger's courage as he guarded his territory from other cats, dogs, and even some humans who appeared to be acting suspiciously!

If only she had such a worthwhile job that required such courage, skill and determination. She was in no doubt at all that

Ginger was probably well rewarded by his owners for such good work!

So, onto the next section! *Please let me score a bit higher on this one,* she thought with a shudder.

Area 6 – Financial Situation

Ok, if she drank the Cream, how would she like this section to look?

Well, obviously she would like to be very wealthy indeed.

But why did she want this?

So she could have a big house, big basket and lots of lovely food of course! Yet, she had seen through completing the other sections of the Wheel that having these things didn't score high in terms of honouring her values and as such weren't high in importance in terms of achieving happiness. However, she conceded that being financially secure could enable her to honour other values such as freedom and family. Yet, she acknowledged that acquiring such material wealth should never be at the *expense* of her freedom and family.

So, overall this section probably wouldn't score any more than 5 in terms of importance for overall happiness.

So, where was she now?

Financially poor. In fact, poor as a church mouse! The only reward she got on a daily basis was a bowl of tuna! Yet, despite this low score, she felt she had no choice but to stay where she was. After all, a bowl of tuna was better than no food at all! So, overall score for this section – 1 for effort!

To summarise:
Current situation: 1 out of 10
Importance for overall happiness: 5 out of 10
Priority for filling this section: Medium

45

Area 7 – Recreation

If she got to drink the Cream, how would she like to spend her free time?

Well, she remembered that she had enjoyed outdoor pursuits when she was a kitten. Yet, what was it about these activities that she had enjoyed?

Thinking back to her kittenhood, she remembered that she had definitely enjoyed the competitive edge of playing chase with the other cats. She had also enjoyed sharing her toys with the others and just basically having fun, particularly running around outside!

So, bearing this in mind, in an ideal world she would be engaging in lots of fun activities with other cats *outside* the house – rather than stuck indoors on her own!

She then reflected that this was yet another section that was very important to her overall happiness. It scored high on her list of values and it was therefore important that it was full, although possibly not quite as high as family life or career. So, probably about 7 out of 10 for importance.

So, where was she now?

Well, basically she had no hobbies or interests. Unless of course you included eating tuna and sleeping! So, how many points did she currently score for this section?

Basically this was another thundering 0.

To her dismay, once again, there appeared to be a pretty big gap between dream and reality.

To summarise:
Current situation: 0
Importance for overall happiness: 7 out of 10
Priority of filling this section: Medium/high

She thought back to the many activities she had witnessed taking place outside her window. *How wonderful it would be to be part of that world again!*

Maybe she would do better in the next section!

Area 8 – Physical Well-being

Right, if she drank the Cream, how would she like to feel and how would she like to look?

Well, for a start, she would like to look in the mirror and feel proud of her reflection! She would see a lean cat with glossy black and white fur. She would wake up in the morning full of energy and feel ready to seize the day! She would have a spring in her step and a glint in her eye! She would feed on a diet rich in variety and flavour. All sorts of food would be available to her – a balanced diet that was healthy and tasty too!

Achieving all of the above was important to her too. So, probably 8 out of 10 in importance to her overall happiness.

So, what was her current situation?

Well, the good news was she was at least in decent health, although *a little overweight*.

Well, if she was honest with herself, *very* overweight!

Yet, despite her not being *ill* as such, she definitely felt lacking in energy. In fact, she would definitely say that she felt tired *most* of the time.

That was probably why she spent most of the day sleeping!

As for feeling proud of her reflection, she tended to avoid mirrors if she could possibly help it. Her once glossy coat was now a dull, matted tangle of fur. The once vibrant ebony was now bleached brown by endless days sitting in the sun, mixed with, dare she say it, the odd premature grey hair! And, was that a flea she saw jumping off, perhaps forced into retreat by the faint whiff of mange?

Of course, she realised that most of her ailments were

47

probably down to lack of exercise, lack of fresh air and too much sleep. Added to that, she felt she could definitely benefit from a more varied diet too.

Surely having only tuna every day couldn't be good for a cat! So what was her current score out of 10?

Unfortunately, probably no more than 2.

To summarise:
Current situation: 2 out of 10
Importance for overall happiness: 8 out of 10
Priority for filling this section: High

She again looked out of the window and was greeted by the sight of Snowy the show cat.

Now there was a sight to behold!

In Serendipity's eyes, Snowy was physical perfection. She was slim with a glossy white coat that seemed to reflect each and every ray of sun now shining down from the sky. She held her head high as she greeted the admiring glances coming from every corner of the lane.

Turning away from the window, Serendipity now felt an urgency to get on to another section of the Wheel so she could complete the task that Polly had set her.

On to the last section! she thought, hoping she could score higher this time.

Area 9 – Emotional/Spiritual Well-being

How would she like to *feel* if she got to drink the Cream of Life?

Again, she thought carefully about how she would like to feel in an ideal world. She had already talked to Polly about her desire to feel more excitement. But what else would she like to feel?

Well ... calm and centred would be good ... gratitude for what she had ... confidence in what she could do ... pride in what she had done.

She then realised that she could add gratitude and confidence to her list of values!

She reflected that this section was probably the most important of all – so 10 out of 10 in importance for achieving overall happiness.

So, what was her current situation?

Well, that was easy. She had no real emotions – apart from boredom of course!

Yet, when she thought about it, that wasn't really true any more. Since meeting Polly she had noticed a new emotion creeping up on her.

That was – dare she say it – excitement!

Although she had to admit that, mixed in with excitement, was another emotion.

That of frustration.

She was starting to acknowledge that this exercise definitely brought out a mixture of the two. Excitement at dreaming about a new life – but frustration at the massive gap between where she was now and where she wanted to be.

So, overall score for this section?

Probably no more than 1.

To summarise:
Current situation: 1 out of 10
Importance for overall happiness: 10 out of 10
Priority for filling this section: Very high

She realised with dismay that this section had the biggest gap yet between importance to her happiness and her current reality.

When she had finished the task, Serendipity let out a huge sigh. So that was it – her Wheel of Life staring back at her!

She could now see that many of the areas most important to her overall happiness were those where she currently scored the lowest. These were therefore the areas she would wish to be filled first when she got to drink the Cream.

After completing this exercise, she felt she needed Polly more than ever to help her find the Dairy. Yet, with a pang of disappointment, she remembered she still had another week before she could see Polly again.

So, the rest of the week went by with Serendipity regularly reviewing her Wheel of Life and dreaming of her new life at the Dairy.

When the night before her meeting with Polly finally arrived, she found it hard to sleep. She was just too excited about seeing the parrot again. So she decided to review what she had learned from her Wheel of Life:

- Some sections were currently fuller than others
- Some sections were more important to honouring her values than others
- The sections that honoured her values were the ones most important for achieving happiness
- For her, these sections were family life, career and emotional well-being
- It was therefore a priority to fill these sections first

When she eventually drifted off to sleep, she dreamed she was at the Celestial Dairy living her ideal life and that her Wheel of Life was now full.

5

'The indispensable first step to getting the things you want out of life is this: decide what you want'[7]

Serendipity awoke with a start. As she yawned and stretched, she began to recall the dream she had had the previous night. It had been a lovely dream where she was now living at the Dairy and leading a perfect life. Although it had been a wonderfully vivid dream she was painfully aware that it had still only been *a dream.*

As she recalled the reality of her current Wheel of Life, she felt a sudden urgency to report back her findings to Polly.

Yet, she knew she would have to wait until her owners had gone out before she dared venture out into the study.

She looked out of the window and saw the sky was dark and overcast.

Looks like rain, she thought.

On most other days, she would have been disappointed by this sort of weather, as it would mean she couldn't lie in the sun.

But not today.

Today all she could think about was getting to see Polly again.

Moments later, she heard a door slam, followed by the sound of a car engine.

Her owners' departure was much earlier than usual.

---

[7] Ben Stein (actor, writer, comedian).

Maybe they wanted to get out before it started to rain. Either way, she considered that it didn't really matter why they had gone out early – the important thing was that the coast was now clear.

At that moment, as if on cue, she heard a shrill whistle coming from next door. So, with great relief, she jumped out of her basket and trotted out into the study.

When she entered the room, Serendipity saw that Polly was sitting upright on her perch staring into space as if in a trance.

Not sure exactly what to say, Serendipity quietly coughed. 'Er, Polly,' she said hesitantly.

Polly looked up abruptly and then appeared to smile...

'Oh, hello Serendipity,' she said, shaking her head. 'I was just day-dreaming! So, how did you get on with your task this week?'

'Well, good ... and bad I suppose,' Serendipity replied cautiously. 'Although, I'm not sure exactly where to start!'

'Start by telling me what was good,' Polly answered reassuringly.

Serendipity paused before replying, carefully considering her response. 'Well, at first it felt great. Breaking my life down into sections was really helpful in identifying exactly how I want my life to look when I get to drink the Cream. I have called this my Wheel of Life.'

Polly nodded as she listened to what Serendipity was saying. 'OK, tell me about your Wheel of Life and how you would like each section to look.'

So, Serendipity went through each section outlining to Polly exactly how she would like her life to be when she got to drink the Cream.

When Serendipity had finished, Polly clapped her wings together enthusiastically. 'Well done, Serendipity. I can see that you have really thought a lot about how you would like your life to be and which areas are most important to your future happiness. Now we need to look at what your life is like at the moment. Hopefully we can then find a way to take you from where you are now to where you want to be.'

'That sounds like a great idea!' Serendipity replied, feeling like an enormous weight had been lifted off her shoulders. 'But where do I start?' she added as she sat down on the floor and crossed her paws.

'How about at the beginning!' replied Polly, hopping onto the swing that was hanging from the roof of her cage.

So, Serendipity began to outline each section of her Wheel of Life, describing in detail what it looked like at the moment.

And Polly listened.

When Serendipity had finished, Polly asked, 'So, how do you feel when you talk about what your life is like at the moment?'

Serendipity looked at the floor and shrugged. 'Pretty sad actually. I guess I really don't like my life very much right now.'

As Serendipity spoke, she realised what a relief it was to finally talk to someone about her life and the emptiness she felt. Up until now, she had just quietly accepted this was the way things were, believing there was nothing she could do to make her life better.

Polly looked at Serendipity with concern. 'Don't worry Serendipity, the important thing is you have taken the first two steps towards improving your life.'

'What are those?' enquired Serendipity, uncrossing her paws as she began to sit up.

Polly smiled and replied, 'The first step is acknowledging you want things to be different. The second is creating a clear picture of how you would like things to be. The next step is to make a plan to ensure that it happens.'

'Sounds good!' Serendipity exclaimed, beginning to feel much more encouraged. 'So, where do we start?'

'Let's start with a specific goal.'

'What's a goal?' enquired Serendipity, realising this was a

word she had not heard before, except from humans when they were watching football.

Polly started to explain. 'In simple terms, a goal is an outcome you want to achieve. You could even call it your "dream" if that makes things easier to understand. You talked yesterday about wanting to get to the Dairy. Is that still your dream?'

'Yes, yes it is!' replied Serendipity excitedly. 'Completing my Wheel of Life has made me more determined than ever to get to the Dairy and to drink the Cream!'

'Right then,' said Polly. 'We now need to make that goal SMART.'

'You mean a *clever* goal?' Serendipity asked tentatively.

'Well, not *clever* exactly. SMART stands for Specific, Measurable, Ambitious, Realistic and Time-specific.'

Serendipity thought for a moment about this explanation before replying, 'OK then, my goal is to *not* stay stuck in my basket any more! How's that?'

'Well, I can see what you are getting at,' replied Polly, 'but unfortunately, you will have to rephrase your goal as you have stated it in the negative.'

Serendipity scratched nervously behind her ear before asking, 'How can *not* staying stuck in my basket be *negative?*'

Polly began to explain. 'It's not the goal itself that's negative, just the way you've phrased it.'

Serendipity appeared to remain confused, despite this explanation. 'I still don't understand,' she said shaking her head and fixing the parrot with a quizzical gaze.

Polly nodded patiently and replied, 'Let me illustrate what I mean. What I want you to do right now is to close your eyes and to *not* think of tuna.'

'Why do you want me to do that?' Serendipity asked, shaking her head again in confusion.

'Don't worry about why,' Polly replied patiently. 'Just close your eyes and *don't* think about tuna.'

'OK,' Serendipity replied and closed her eyes. It wasn't long before a frown appeared on her face.

'So, what did you think of?' asked Polly.

Serendipity shook her head once more and cautiously replied, 'Er . . . tuna!'

'But, why did you think of tuna when I specifically asked you not to?'

'I tried not to, but it just popped into my head!' replied Serendipity with her paws outstretched in resignation.

'Exactly!' laughed Polly. 'It's a fact of life that our brains cannot visualise a negative such as *not* or *don't*. So, instead it focuses on the main information-carrying word. In your case that all important word was tuna! When you say your goal is "*Not* to stay stuck in your basket", your mind is forced to focus on the words *stuck* and *basket*! However, what we want your brain to focus on is what you *do* want rather than what you *don't* want.'

'Right, I think I understand now,' replied Serendipity, beginning to feel more confident with this explanation.

She took a few moments to think about a new, positively phrased goal. 'Right then . . . what I *do* want is to live an exciting and fulfilling life!'

'That's much better,' replied Polly. 'However, it's still a bit vague. We now need to make it more specific.'

'I don't quite see how it can be vague,' said Serendipity, cocking her head to one side and scratching behind her ear. 'I *specifically* want to feel more excited and fulfilled!'

'Let me explain,' replied Polly. 'You need to make a goal *specific* in order to be able to measure your success in achieving it and also to be able to *visualise* yourselves achieving it.'

'Right, I *think* I see what you mean,' replied Serendipity, still feeling a little perplexed. However, she took her time to think about what she thought was a new, more specific goal. 'OK then, my goal is to get to the Dairy. Is that specific enough?'

'Yes, that is!' laughed Polly. 'Now, the next step it to make it *measurable.* To do this, we need to look at how you will *know* you have successfully achieved your goal.'

'Well, that's pretty obvious,' replied Serendipity. 'When I get to the Dairy, of course!'

Polly shook her head. 'Yes, but I need a *more* detailed picture from you. Remember, it's *your* goal so it's *you* who needs to define exactly what you mean by success.'

Serendipity thought carefully about what Polly had just said before giving her reply.

'Well, I guess it would be no good getting to the Dairy and not being welcomed there. And it would be no good being welcomed there if I didn't get to drink the Cream. Yet, it would be no good drinking the Cream if my Wheel of Life was still empty. So ... I guess ... I would feel successful if I got to the Dairy, got to drink the Cream and at least three quarters of my Wheel of Life was then full.'

Polly nodded and said, 'Great, we now know exactly what it is you want to achieve when you get there. Now we need to make your goal "time-specific". So, when exactly would you like to get to the Dairy?'

Serendipity looked at Polly with confusion. 'Hold on, what about the Ambitious and Realistic bit?'

Polly nodded patiently and replied, 'We will come to that later. For the moment we need to think about a specific time-scale. Remember, a goal is a *dream with a date.* So, when do you want to get to the Dairy?'

'Well,' exclaimed Serendipity, 'as soon as possible, of course!'

Polly shook her head. 'That's not specific enough. I need a *definite* date you can work towards. So, when *exactly* do you plan to get there?'

Serendipity was sure she wanted to get there quickly so replied, 'OK, how about next week?'

'How realistic do you feel that timescale is?' replied Polly, ruffling her tail feathers.

As Serendipity thought carefully about this question, she

realised that so far she hadn't even got outside the house, let alone found directions to get to the Dairy. Considering how far away the Dairy looked from her window, she couldn't *really* see how she could get there any time soon.

So she replied, 'Well ... I suppose that isn't very realistic is it?'

'So what timescale do you feel would be more realistic?' replied Polly patiently.

Serendipity pondered this question. 'Well, I suppose a more realistic date would be some time next year.'

Polly nodded and then asked, 'How challenging do you feel that timescale is?'

Serendipity frowned. 'Why does it have to be challenging?'

'In order for you to achieve your goal, your timescale needs to be challenging as well as realistic. If a timescale is too far in the distance, it won't feel that challenging and you are more likely to lose interest in achieving your goal.'

'Well, I could make it more challenging by moving the timescale forward but then it might become less realistic.'

'So what timescale would feel realistic yet still challenging to you?'

Serendipity again thought carefully before answering.

'Well, I suppose maybe if I gave myself six weeks to get to the Dairy, it would still seem challenging but it would give me enough time to prepare for the trip. So, that would make it more realistic too! I would need to start my trip before winter sets in ... so six weeks should give me enough time.'

'Great!' exclaimed Polly. 'So, how ambitious does that goal now feel?'

'Why does it need to be ambitious?' asked Serendipity.

'Well, in order to have a high chance of achieving a goal, you need to feel really excited about the outcome. Goals that don't really get the juices flowing are often abandoned before they really get going!'

Serendipity sighed a big sigh. 'That's the thing,' she

explained. 'It feels *very* ambitious and the outcome feels very exciting indeed. Yet ... it's one thing talking about getting to the Dairy but, deep down, it doesn't really feel achievable.'

'What might stop it being achievable?'

'Well, for a start, the Dairy is so far, far away. So far away that, if I'm honest, I could never *really* dream of getting there.'

'But you *have* dreamed about it and you said it felt good!'

'Yes, but it looks such a long way away, I just couldn't possibly travel that far, I don't have a clue how to get there so I would probably get lost and ... well ... it's all very well talking about getting to the Dairy and drinking the Cream but ... when I get there the other cats probably won't like me anyway, or will just ignore me, and well, even if they didn't ignore me, they probably wouldn't let me near the Cream and ... '

Serendipity paused and looked down at the ground.

'Yes, go on,' Polly said gently.

Serendipity looked up at the parrot, but suddenly felt too embarrassed to carry on.

Polly merely said, 'Don't worry Serendipity, just take your time.'

'Well,' stammered Serendipity, bracing herself for the words to follow. 'I'm too big to fit through the cat flap! So I wouldn't even be able to get as far as the front door, let alone travel the long, hard journey to the Dairy!'

As Polly listened, she nodded sympathetically. 'Right, you have just given me an awful lot of obstacles to achieving your goal of getting to the Dairy and drinking the cream. We need to make a note of these obstacles because we will look at these in more detail later. But for now, what I want you to do is to concentrate on succeeding in your goal rather than looking for possible reasons for failure.'

'But how do I do that when I'm facing all these obstacles?' asked Serendipity with a big sigh.

'Well, you need to start programming your brain for success by visualising yourself succeeding in your goal,' replied Polly.

'What I want you to do now is to close your eyes and create the most detailed image possible of yourself getting to the Dairy and drinking the Cream. You need to think about what you are doing, how you are feeling and what others around you are saying. Make the colours bright, the feelings strong and the sounds loud and clear. Don't worry too much at the moment about *how* you are going to get to the Dairy, just concentrate on the outcome you want.'

'That sounds like a great idea,' said Serendipity, and began to close her eyes. However, just at that moment she heard a car outside and realised that her owners must have returned.

'I think I had better go now and get started on that visualisation task!' said Serendipity with a sense of urgency. 'I will practise that every morning from now on!'

'Before you go,' said Polly, 'I just need you to check that your goal is still compatible with your core values.'

'My core values?'

'Yes, when you talked about the times you were most happy, you highlighted a list of values that you held dear. I need you to remind me of what they were so we can check they are compatible with your goal of getting to the Dairy and drinking the cream.'

So, Serendipity went over her list of core values:

What she valued in her life

* A challenge
* A sense of purpose
* A sense of achievement
* A sense of responsibility
* A sense of belonging
* A sense of community
* Independence
* Excitement
* Fun

59

* Family
* Harmony
* Helping others
* Sharing with others
* Feeling loved
* Freedom of choice
* Variety

What she valued in herself and others

* Generosity
* Kindness
* Friendship
* Loyalty
* Trust
* Integrity
* Positivity
* Gratitude
* Confidence
* Respect
* Work ethic

As Serendipity went through her list of values, she was immediately filled with a sense of pride and joy. She then thought about which sections of her Wheel of Life she would fill up first and how important these sections were for achieving happiness.

Serendipity smiled and said to Polly, 'Yes, I can honestly say that by getting to the Dairy and drinking the Cream, I would be honouring each and every one of these values.'

'That's excellent!' replied Polly, 'you've done some brilliant work today! Now remember, every day this week, make sure you practise visualising the outcome you want from your goal. The more you practise this, the more excited you will become – and the more likely you will be to succeed!'

'Yes, I will definitely practise my visualisation several times a day,' Serendipity replied excitedly. 'I will practise it first thing in the morning, once during the day and once before I go to sleep!'

'That sounds great Serendipity!' Polly enthused, clapping her wings together. 'Good luck and see you next week!'

'See you then!' Serendipity replied and quickly scrambled back to her basket.

When she got back to the conservatory, her mind was literally buzzing with excitement. She couldn't wait to try out the visualisation task that Polly had set her. So she climbed into her basket and began to visualise what it would be like to achieve her goal of getting to the Dairy and drinking the Cream.

Settling into the cosy bedding, she let her mind relax and slowly but surely an image began to form in her mind.

At first, the magical farm and the Dairy were just mere spots in the distance. Yet, as she got nearer, she became aware of the treat that was in store for each and every one of her senses.

She saw the sun shining brightly in the sky, its rays reflecting off the brilliant sheen of the grass in the surrounding fields. She saw the flowers and the hedgerows illuminating the magical farm with their bright and vibrant colours. She heard the rustling of the leaves on the elegant trees as they swayed gently in the breeze.

This was paradise indeed.

She smelt the sweet scent of the meadow surrounding the Dairy and, as she got nearer, became aware of the intoxicating aroma of freshly churned cream.

She felt the warmth of the sun on her face tempered by the cooling breeze, and was filled with a surge of excitement and pride as she approached the entrance to the Dairy.

As she entered, she was enveloped in a welcome so warm she could feel the love of each and every cat that had gathered there to greet her.

As she drank the Cream of Life that was waiting for her in a bowl with her name on it, she was treated to a taste sensation that had to be experienced to be believed.

As her tummy filled up with the Cream, she could feel her Wheel of Life filling up too.

Yet, she stopped short of finishing the whole bowl, as she wanted to make sure there was plenty to share with the other cats, who she now thought of as part of her family.

Besides, she wasn't greedy, as she knew she had reached her goal of a Wheel of Life that was now three-quarters full!

The more detailed she made the image, the more her feelings of excitement grew and the more determined she became to achieve her goal of getting to the Dairy and drinking the Cream.

Her goal was definitely beginning to feel ambitious yet, at the same time, achievable too!

As she settled into her basket for the night, Serendipity carefully considered what she had learned so far:

- ❧ She had acknowledged that her life wasn't that great and there were things she wanted to change
- ❧ She had developed a detailed picture of what she would like her life to be like and what was most important to her overall happiness. She had set a goal which was SMART: Specific, Measurable, Ambitious, Realistic and Time-specific.
- ❧ The more exciting the goal, the more likely she was to succeed
- ❧ She got excited by visualising herself achieving her goal
- ❧ Visualisation made the goal feel more achievable too!
- ❧ She had checked that achieving her goal was compatible with her core values and was therefore likely to contribute to her future happiness

The rest of the week flew by with Serendipity regularly practising visualising her goal of getting to the Dairy. As promised, she practised this three times a day. Each time she practise it, the more exciting the goal became and the more she began to really believe she could achieve it.

By the end of the week, she was itching to see Polly again to tell her about her achievements!

The night before she was due to see Polly, she once again dreamed of the magical place where she knew all her dreams would come true.

6

'Don't be afraid of the space between your dreams and reality. If you can dream it you can make it so'[8]

Serendipity awoke with an unusual feeling of well-being. She looked out of the window and saw that the sun was already quite high in the sky.

For a moment she was confused about where she was. She knew that she felt warm and comfortable, but where exactly was she?

As she recalled the details of the previous night's dream, she felt a flood of excitement flow through her body.

Yes, she remembered now.

She was at the Dairy! Her Wheel of Life was three-quarters full and so was her tummy!

Yes, it was three-quarters full of the Cream of Life!

She then heard a rumble and wondered where it might be coming from. Was it perhaps coming from outside?

She looked out of the window and again noticed that the sun was shining high in the sky.

She concluded that the sound was definitely not coming from outside.

On hearing the sound again, she couldn't help but notice that it was coming from much closer than she had originally thought. So close in fact that she could actually *feel* it!

---

[8] Belva Davis (broadcaster and journalist).

To her surprise, she realised that the sound was not coming from outside at all, but from inside her tummy! Yet, it was not the rumble from a tummy that was three-quarters full – but the rumble from an empty one.

A very empty one indeed!

She then looked around and to her disappointment realised that she was not in fact at the Dairy but still stuck in her old basket!

While coming to terms with her disappointment, she heard another rumble.

But this time it was not coming from inside her tummy.

Looking outside, she saw that the sun had now disappeared behind the big black clouds that were rapidly gathering in the sky.

It looked like the day was not going to turn out as sunny as she had first thought.

In fact, it definitely looked like she was in for some rain.

It then occurred to her that a week of visualising her goal must have prompted the vivid dream she had experienced the night before.

However, she was now faced with the reality of being stuck in her old basket and was instantly reminded of how far she still had to go to get to where she wanted to be.

As she pondered this reality, she heard a whistle from next door.

Time to see Polly again!

When she entered the study, she was shocked to see Polly lying on her back with her legs in the air.

Desperate to see if Polly was all right, she rushed up to the cage, concern etched all over her face. Yet, just as she was about to say Polly's name, Serendipity was amazed to see the parrot suddenly perform a 180-degree back flip before landing steadily on her feet.

Despite her shock at this sudden acrobatic feat, Serendipity was glad to see her friend clearly alive and well. Letting out a huge sigh of relief she exclaimed, 'Polly, I was so worried, I thought you might be dead when I saw you lying there on your back!'

Yet, Polly simply replied, 'Perception is not always reality my dear Serendipity. Perception is not always reality.'

Before Serendipity had time to reply to this cryptic statement, Polly jumped back onto her perch and said excitedly, 'So how did you get on with your task for this week?'

'Well,' replied Serendipity with a tentative smile, 'I have been practising visualising my goal on a regular basis. I do this first thing in the morning, several times during the day, and just before I go to bed. At first I found it hard to get a detailed image in my mind, but now I find it quite easy and am filled with a wonderful sense of excitement every time I do it. The image in my mind is now so clear that it sparked off the most wonderfully vivid dream last night.'

'Tell me more,' enquired Polly with great interest.

'Well, I dreamed that I was already at the Dairy, I had drunk the Cream and my Wheel of Life was now three-quarters full. But then ... '

Serendipity paused, looked at the ground and felt a lump begin to form in her throat.

Polly looked at Serendipity with concern. 'Yes, Serendipity, tell me what happened next.'

So Serendipity continued, 'Well, when I woke up I realised that, in reality, my life wasn't like that at all. I wasn't at the Dairy, but stuck in my old basket, looking out of the window and watching the world and my life pass me by.'

Polly merely nodded. 'Don't worry,' she said. 'This is all part of the process of working towards your goal. You see, in order to get to where you want to be, you first need to confront the reality of where you are right now. We have so far looked in detail at your goal and what you want to achieve. We now need to look more closely at what is currently happening with your life.'

'Why do we need to do that?' replied Serendipity, feeling somewhat confused.

Polly nodded patiently. 'Well, we need to look at where you are right now in order to identify the obstacles you may have to face on your journey to reaching your goal – and to identify the resources that will help you to overcome them.'

Serendipity was intrigued by what Polly was saying. 'OK, so, how exactly are we going to do that?' she asked.

'Well,' said Polly, 'let's go back to your Wheel of Life and look at what is good that is happening right now. This will give you an idea of the resources currently available to help you get to where you want to be.'

So, Serendipity once again went through her Wheel of Life and reflected on where she was right now. Although she could see there was still a long way to go before she got to where she wanted to be, she had to admit there were also some things that were good about her life at the moment.

* She still had her health
* She was still *reasonably* young
* She had a family of sorts
* She had a roof over her head and food to eat
* She had a job of sorts so at least had *some* work experience behind her
* She also had some experience of having fun from when she was a kitten
* She did have moments of contentment, even though it *was* just lying in the sun!

When she had finished the list, she had to admit to feeling a *little* better about where she was right now.

'Well done!' exclaimed Polly, clapping her wings together. 'We can look at this list again later when we consider possible resources to help you get to the Dairy. However, the next question I need to ask you is this.

'What have you done so far to make things the way you want them to be?'

Serendipity was a little thrown by this question. Cocking her head to one side she replied cautiously, 'Well, er . . . nothing.'

'What, *nothing*?' challenged Polly.

Serendipity thought carefully before replying. 'Well, I *suppose* talking to you about my dreams is a start.'

'Yes, that's definitely a good start but, what in the past stopped you from doing more to make your life better?'

Serendipity shook her head in frustration. 'There just didn't seem any point.'

'What do you mean by *no point*?'

'Well, I suppose I just never thought that things could ever be different. I never thought there was anything I could do to make my life better, so I never took the time to think about how things could change. I guess I just quietly accepted this was what my life was like and would be forever more, amen.'

'So, how do you feel now?' asked Polly, ruffling her feathers.

'Well,' replied Serendipity, 'I now have a clear picture of what I would like my life to be like and this has given me the will and determination to really do something about it.'

'Well done, Serendipity,' said Polly bobbing her head up and down. 'We now need to look at what you feel might *stop* you from achieving your goal of getting to the Dairy and drinking the Cream.'

'Er . . . I don't know what might stop me,' replied Serendipity, suddenly feeling a little embarrassed.

'Well, you came up with quite a long list the other day,' said Polly, casually preening her feathers.

Serendipity squirmed uncomfortably. 'Er . . . I think you will have to remind me of what they were,' she replied tentatively.

So, Polly outlined the obstacles that Serendipity had previously mentioned.

1. You don't know how to get to the Dairy

2. The Dairy is too far away and you could never travel that far
3. You are too big to get through the cat flap
4. The other cats might not like you when you get there

When Polly had listed these obstacles, Serendipity felt more than a little uncomfortable about what she had just heard. She couldn't help but wonder how she would ever overcome all these obstacles and get to where she wanted to be.

However, Polly sounded in determined mood. 'Right now,' she said, with her wings outstretched, 'let's look at these obstacles one by one and see if we can come up with some ways to help you overcome them.'

'OK,' said Serendipity a little reluctantly.

'Right,' said Polly. 'Let's start with the first obstacle: you don't know how to get to the Dairy. What could you do to overcome that one?'

Serendipity twitched her ears as she carefully considered her reply.

'Well, I guess I would need to find out exactly where the Dairy is.'

'So, how would you go about doing that?'

'Well, I don't have a map so I would need to ask someone.'

'So, who would you ask?'

Serendipity looked out of the window in the hope it would give her some answers. 'Well, I guess I would need to ask another cat. Most cats have heard about the Dairy so there must be someone who could give me directions.'

Polly nodded in agreement. 'Great. That's a good start. Now, what about the next obstacle: the Dairy is too far away and you could never travel that far. What could you do to overcome that one?'

Serendipity again thought carefully before replying.

'Well, I suppose if I knew where the Dairy was, I would have a better idea of how far I would have to travel and could therefore plan my journey accordingly. I could also make sure I was fit so I could travel a long distance if necessary!'

Polly nodded again before replying, 'Well done, Serendipity. That sounds great. So, how about the third obstacle – you are too big to get through the cat flap.'

This obstacle was particularly difficult for Serendipity to talk about, so she said quietly, 'Well, I suppose I should try out the cat flap first to see if I can get through and if not then I could go on a diet to lose some weight and then I might *just* be able to squeeze through!'

Polly nodded and clapped her wings together. 'Sounds great, Serendipity! So, what about the final obstacle – that the other cats might not like you when you get to the Dairy?'

Serendipity looked down at the ground and shifted her body uncomfortably. She tried to speak but no words would come out.

'What's wrong, Serendipity?' asked Polly with concern.

'Well, to be honest with you,' she replied in no more than whisper, 'I'm afraid they might laugh at me because of my weight. But I *suppose* I could *try* to talk to the other cats in the lane and see if they like me. If *they* like me then the cats at the Dairy might like me too.'

'You *suppose* you could *try* to talk to other cats?' asked Polly.

Serendipity laughed at the way Polly had challenged her use of words. 'Yes, Polly, when I get outside the cat flap I will *definitely* talk to the other cats!'

Polly joined in with the laughter. 'Great – you have come up with some wonderful ideas! Let's now look at some of the resources you already have to help you to get to the Dairy.'

Serendipity thought about the ideas she had already come up with and saw that, despite her initial doubts, she did in fact have *some* resources to help her achieve her goal. So she began to explain to Polly what these resources were.

'Well, I can already see the smoke which could help me to navigate my way to the Dairy and I also know there are plenty of other cats who might know the way there. Also, I have already visualised getting to the Dairy so this has given me the determination to succeed.'

Polly looked impressed with what she had just heard.

'That's great Serendipity! Those are some great resources indeed! So, what other resources will you need to get you there?'

Serendipity thought for a moment before replying tentatively, 'Well, I guess I will need to find someone to go with me as I would rather not travel alone.'

She paused for a moment in order to collect her thoughts. Inspired by some new ideas she continued. 'I will also need some definite directions, more fitness and more stamina.'

'Another great answer!' exclaimed Polly encouragingly. 'Now we need to put together an action plan based on the resources you already have and the ones you will need to get. To start with, I want you to brainstorm as many options you can think of that will help you to get to the Dairy. Remember to use the ideas you have already come up with to help you. Take your time, let your mind run free and don't hold back.'

As Serendipity tried to think of specific actions to overcome the obstacles she faced, her mind drew a blank.

In fact, the more she tried to think of some answers, the more blank her mind became.

'I can't think of anything,' Serendipity finally said, shaking her head with frustration.

'Not to worry,' replied Polly reassuringly. 'Let me ask you this:

What if time weren't a factor and you didn't have to live with the consequences of your actions – what would you do then?'

To her surprise, Serendipity realised that this question seemed to put a different perspective on things.

Thinking about her options from this angle, she continued

with increasing confidence. 'Well, I suppose if I didn't have to live with the consequences and I had all the time in the world ... then I would probably go and visit every cat in the street ... no ... every cat in the *world* and ask them if they knew where the Dairy was. I wouldn't care if they told me to go away or said they didn't know the answer because I would just go and ask someone else instead, and it wouldn't matter how long it took as I would have all the time in the world!'

As she started to think about what options were available when she didn't worry about the consequences, more ideas started to form in her mind.

'Go on,' said Polly with encouragement. 'What if money weren't a factor?'

'Right, if money weren't a factor I would give up my job as a mouser and devote all my time to getting to the Dairy. I would hire the best personal trainer to help me get slim and fit, and, I would eat only the leanest meat to help build up my strength. I would then easily be able to slide through the cat flap and have the stamina to get to the Dairy.'

To her delight, Serendipity realised that when she let her mind run free without any restrictions on her imagination, more and more ideas came flooding to her.

So she continued with increasing excitement.

'Let's see ... I would get up at the crack of dawn, jump out of my basket, push my way through the cat flap, run through the garden, jump over the wall, swim every river, run down every valley, scale every hill, and then lead an army of cats to help me seek out the Dairy!'

Polly could see the excitement growing on Serendipity's face as she came up with more and more ideas to help her get to the Dairy. 'Well done, Serendipity!' she said. 'That's a great list! Now, let's look at some of those ideas and see how many we can use to put together a specific action plan to help you get to the Dairy.'

'OK, Polly,' enthused Serendipity, still on a high from the list of options she had just come up with. 'That sounds like a great idea!'

So, she began to think about which of these ideas she could use to put together an action plan for getting to the Dairy.

'Right,' she said, 'I would get up much earlier in the morning and devote some specific time to planning my trip, lose some weight so I can get through the cat flap, ask some of the other cats how to get to the Dairy, plan a route, get fit by eating healthily and take more exercise in preparation for the long trip ahead.'

When Serendipity had finished her list, Polly looked impressed. 'OK, from the list you have just given me, what specific actions are you going to take first?'

Serendipity thought for a minute and, to her great disappointment, again felt her mind go blank. 'Er,' she replied, 'I'm not really sure where to start.'

'OK then,' said Polly. 'Which actions from your list do you think will be the easiest and would help you take that first step to achieving your goal of getting to the Dairy and drinking the Cream?'

Serendipity again went through her list of options and, as she did so, could gradually feel the fog beginning to clear in her mind.

'Well, if you put it like that,' she said, 'probably the first step would be to put together a specific plan outlining the actions I would need to take to get to the Dairy. I've given myself six weeks to get there so I need to know *exactly* what I hope to achieve each week. Breaking down my goal into bite-sized tasks will make it seem much more achievable too! I could also visualise each step of my journey to make a sort of map in my mind. I found visualising my goal really useful so I could add to that by making a movie in my mind outlining my path to success!'

'Sounds great!' exclaimed Polly. 'What else could you do that would help you take that first step towards getting to the Dairy?'

Again, Serendipity thought carefully before replying. 'Well, I could also reduce my food intake by eating only half a bowl instead of a whole bowl of tuna. This would help me lose some weight so I could get through the cat flap!'

As Serendipity talked about what would help her to take those first few steps towards getting to the Dairy, more and more ideas began to come to her.

So, she continued. 'I could also start exercising which would help me to lose even more weight and get fit for the journey to the Dairy. I could start off by doing just a few press-ups which would be fairly easy and would definitely help me take those first few steps forward!'

Serendipity looked over at Polly and could see that she was impressed with these answers.

'Those are excellent ideas, Serendipity – well done!' she exclaimed. 'Now, let's look again at those options. When *exactly* are you going to start putting together your action plan and begin practising your visualisation task?'

'Oh, I will do that this afternoon,' replied Serendipity, matter-of-factly.

'When *exactly* this afternoon?' enquired Polly.

'Good point!' laughed Serendipity. 'Well, as soon as my owners get back and I have to leave this room!'

'What about rationing your food and beginning your exercises?'

'Oh, probably tomorrow!' sighed Serendipity.

'*Probably* tomorrow?' challenged Polly.

'No, *definitely* tomorrow!' replied Serendipity with a laugh, getting used to Polly's style of questioning.

'That's more like it!' Polly laughed back. 'Now, what time *specifically* are you going to get up?'

'Well, I normally don't get up until about 11 a.m. on a

Monday morning but in order to get going with my actions I will try to get up by 8 a.m.'

'*Try* to get up at 8 a.m.?' enquired Polly.

'No, I *will* get up at 8 a.m. and then begin my actions immediately after that!' laughed Serendipity, feeling grateful to Polly for challenging her to be more specific.

'Great!' exclaimed Polly. 'Now, the next thing we need to do is to check out your commitment to these actions. After all, it's one thing saying you are going to do something, but being really *committed* to doing it is another thing altogether! So, on a scale of 1 to 10, how committed are you to doing these things?'

'What do you mean by *committed*?' asked Serendipity, eyeing up the bars on Polly's cage. 'The only time I've heard that term is when humans talk about being committed to some sort of prison for the insane!'

Polly laughed. 'Well, it *would* be insane to say you're going to do something without being committed! But seriously, when I ask how committed you are, I'm really asking you how *sure* you are that you will carry out these actions.'

'Oh, I'm very *sure* I want to do these things!' Serendipity replied confidently. 'So I would say my score was 10 out of 10 for commitment!'

Yet, as Serendipity began to think more carefully about carrying out these particular actions, she realised that the question of commitment wasn't quite as easy as she had first thought.

If she was being honest with herself, how much did she *really* want to have to get up early tomorrow morning or to spend this afternoon writing an action plan?

So, with this in mind she added, 'Well, to be honest with you, on reflection it's probably only about 7 out of 10.'

'What stops it being 10?'

'Well, I *do* think it would make sense to do these things but, you know, getting up early tomorrow morning might be really hard, especially if it's cold outside or raining and ... well ... if the weather is warm this afternoon, I might be tempted to just lie in the sun rather than sweating over an action plan!'

Polly nodded sympathetically. 'I can quite understand how hard this must seem but let me ask you this: *What will happen if you don't follow through with these actions?*'

Serendipity pondered this question for a few moments and then replied, 'I will stay exactly where I am and will never get to the Dairy?'

'And how would that make you feel?'

When Serendipity thought about how this would feel she replied in a quiet voice, 'Pretty disappointed with myself and ... well ... if I'm really honest, pretty depressed actually.'

'And how would you feel if you *did* follow through with these actions?' asked Polly.

'Oh, that would be completely different!' replied Serendipity, immediately feeling better. 'Well, in fact, I would feel really good, proud and ... excited!'

'So,' said Polly, 'with this in mind, how committed are you now to following through with your actions?'

When Serendipity considered the contrast between how she would feel if she *did* take action and how she would feel if she *didn't* take action, she immediately felt much more confident that she would indeed carry out these actions.

'Well, if you put it that way,' she replied, 'my commitment is probably now 10 out of 10.'

'*Probably* 10 out of 10?'

'No, *definitely* 10 out of 10!' Serendipity exclaimed triumphantly.

And they both laughed out loud.

When they had finished laughing, Polly said, 'Well, it sounds like you have a lot to be getting on with. I'm sure when we meet next week you will have lots of wonderful things to report!'

Although Serendipity felt sad that she would not be seeing Polly again for another week, she knew that she needed this time to get on with all her plans. Besides, she knew she would have to develop some self-reliance if she was going to get herself to the Dairy.

'OK, Polly,' she said resolutely. 'I will get on with these actions each day this week and by the time I next see you, I intend to have lost at least one pound in weight!'

'Wow, sounds like you have an exciting and challenging week ahead!' exclaimed Polly.

And again, they both laughed.

At that moment, they heard the familiar sound of a car approaching.

'Looks like your owners are back,' said Polly. 'Best of luck with your plans – and see you the same time next week.'

'OK, Polly, will do – and thanks!' said Serendipity with a wave of her paw.

'You're welcome!' replied Polly, as she also waved goodbye.

Serendipity then quickly scampered back to the conservatory and settled down once more into her basket.

She realised she was just in time as, right at that moment, she saw her owners come sweeping in through the door.

As Serendipity lay in her basket pretending to be asleep, she heard a voice say scornfully, 'No guesses how many mice she's caught today!'

Serendipity then heard footsteps disappearing into the room next door and realised she was alone once more.

She considered that there *was* a time when such a comment would have hurt her. However, right at that moment, Serendipity didn't really care what her owners thought about her. The only thing on her mind right now was getting to the Dairy and drinking the Cream.

Besides, the only person she really cared about now was Polly. Unlike her owners, Polly genuinely seemed to want the best for her. Serendipity considered how great it felt to have someone who was actually supporting her rather than judging her.

That certainly hadn't happened for a long, long time.

For the rest of the day, Serendipity's mind was buzzing. Even though the sun had now come out and she was very tempted to sunbathe, she really wanted to get going with writing her action plan for getting to the Dairy. Recalling her owner's comments, she reluctantly considered it might be a good idea to perhaps try to catch some mice first. However, catching mice held no appeal for her, especially not today. Sometimes she would do a short hunt in the morning and maybe another in the afternoon. Yet, there was usually no real incentive for her as, despite their earlier comments, her owners never seemed to notice what she did anyway!

Serendipity had never found her job exactly *inspiring*. Yet, talking to Polly had made her realise how totally boring and meaningless her work actually was and how there were so many other more exciting things she could be doing with her life instead!

So, spurred on by this thought, she decided she would spend the rest of the afternoon getting on with her action plan and then, if she had time, she would have a quick look round for some mice.

She considered this would be a *sort* of compromise.

So, getting into a comfortable position in her basket, she began to put together a plan for the six weeks that lay ahead.

Firstly, she thought back to the options that she had outlined to Polly.

Right, she thought, *I have six weeks to get to the Dairy. What do I need to do to enable me to get there?* She then listed her options:

1. Lose weight so I can fit through the cat flap
2. Get outside the cat flap
3. Find out where the Dairy is
4. Plan a route
5. Find a more balanced diet
6. Get fit for the long journey ahead

If I break this down into weekly tasks, she thought, *I will need to do the following*:

Week 1
Reduce food intake
Begin daily exercises
Lose 1 lb

Week 2
Increase daily exercises
Get outside the cat flap
Lose 1 lb

Week 3
Find out where the Dairy is and plan a route
Find a more balanced diet
Lose 1 lb

Week 4
Begin exercising outside
Do at least 10 laps of the garden per day
Lose 1 lb

Week 5
Increase to at least 20 laps of the garden per day
Lose 1 lb

Week 6
Get over the wall and start recruiting other cats to join me on my journey
Lose 2 lbs

When she had completed this task, Serendipity decided to write it all out in the form of a table so she could see at a glance what she was aiming to achieve each week. Breaking her goal into bite-sized chunks instantly made getting to the Dairy seem much more achievable. When she had finished, her action plan looked something like this:

	Week 1	Week 2	Week 3	Week 4	Week 5	Week 6
Action	Get up at 8 a.m. Eat only half a bowl of tuna per day Start exercising: 10 press-ups per day	Get outside cat flap Continue rationing food Increase to 20 press-ups per day	Find directions to Dairy and plan route Find a more balanced diet 20 press-ups per day	Start exercising outside 20 press-ups per day At least 10 laps of garden per day	20 press-ups per day Do at least 20 laps of the garden per day	Get over the wall Start recruiting other cats Begin journey to Dairy
Target weight	14 lbs	13 lbs	12lbs	11 lbs	10 lbs	8 lbs

When Serendipity had completed this task she felt a sense of quiet satisfaction with what she had achieved and couldn't wait to show her plan to Polly.

However, the rest of the afternoon drifted by uneventfully, with the usual drudgery of trekking off to search around the house for mice.

As usual there were *none* to be seen.

As Serendipity settled down for the night she reviewed what she had learned so far that day:

❧ Despite her general dissatisfaction, there were already some things about her life that were good
❧ These were resources that could help her to get to the Dairy
❧ She had identified what obstacles might lie ahead
❧ She had come up with some ideas about how to get over these obstacles
❧ She had broken these ideas down into specific actions and come up with a timetable for achieving her goal

81

❧ Breaking her goal into bite-sized tasks had immediately made it seem more achievable
❧ She had then imagined each stage of her journey using her now powerful skills of visualisation
❧ She could instantly see exactly what she needed to do to get to the Dairy and imagined how good it would feel to achieve each step

Serendipity then made a pledge to herself that each day when she got up she would look at her action plan to remind herself of what she needed to do to get to the Dairy. She would then visualise herself taking the required actions to get there.

Finally, she would visualise herself achieving her goal and imagine how good it would feel.

She realised that she would need to get a good night's sleep tonight as the following morning she was due to take the next step of getting up early and rationing her food.

That night, as she slept, Serendipity dreamed she was a film star featuring in the movie of her life. The movie told the story of how, one day, she found the courage to leave the comfort of her basket and begin the long, hard journey to the Dairy – and how all her dreams came true when she got there.

7

'If you want the rainbow, you've got to put up with a little rain' [9]

When Serendipity awoke from a blissful sleep, she was greeted to the sound of rain beating down on the window pane.

All thoughts of dreams and magic momentarily vanished.

Serendipity considered how it had suddenly got *very* cold. She felt a shiver run through her body as her nose touched the window and a blast of cold air shot through a small crack that had suddenly appeared in the corner of the glass.

Instinctively she retreated deeper into her basket until the familiar warmth once again surrounded her.

She looked at the clock and saw it was 8 o'clock. *Just five more minutes in my basket before I brave the cold* she thought, and instantly felt better.

Five minutes soon turned into ten and, before she knew it, 8 o'clock had turned to 9 o'clock, 9 o'clock had turned to 10 o'clock and 10 o'clock had turned to 11 o'clock.

The earlier feelings of comfort she had experienced from her lie-in soon turned to intense *discomfort*.

She hadn't done what she had set out to do that morning.

She looked over to the bowl of tuna that had been left, predictably, next to her basket.

---

[9] Dolly Parton (singer, songwriter, actress, author).

She recalled how eating only half a bowl was an important task for her this morning.

Yet, feeling so disappointed with herself for not getting up early, she felt like eating all the food just to help take away the feelings of guilt.

She knew she had nearly a week before she saw Polly again – so that gave her six more mornings to reach her target weight. She reasoned that, as it was cold today, it had been difficult to get up anyway.

It would probably be warmer tomorrow so it would be easier then.

That meant it made much more sense to start rationing her food and beginning her exercises tomorrow!

Yes, the more she thought about it, the more this made sense.

She would begin her tasks tomorrow instead.

When she had made this decision, she instantly felt much better. She could feel it was getting warmer now so, before she had time to change her mind, she got out of her basket, went straight over to the bowl and scoffed all the tuna.

She had been hoping that eating the whole bowl would make her feel better – but all it did was make her feel sick.

This really brought home to her how disappointed she was with herself for failing both her tasks that morning.

How would she ever get to the Dairy now – and what would Polly say?

At this point, Serendipity even considered lying to her friend and pretending that she had achieved her goals today. Yet, deep down she knew that the only person she was really letting down was herself. Besides, something told her that Polly would probably see through her lies anyway!

No, she would just have to come clean and tell her the truth.

And this just depressed her even more.

So, for the rest of the day Serendipity just sat in her basket and even gave up on her afternoon mouse hunt. What was the point anyway?

Yet, despite what had happened that morning, Serendipity still knew that she had to hold on to her dream of getting to the Dairy. So she decided she would *definitely* get up early tomorrow and begin her new diet and exercise routine then.

However, the next morning it was even colder than the day before. So cold in fact that Serendipity couldn't bear to even stick so much as her nose out of her basket until the room had begun to significantly warm up – which was two hours later!

When she finally got up, she felt the same feelings of failure starting to overwhelm her once more.

Looking over at her bowl of food, she realised she just couldn't face the thought of only eating half of it. Besides, she had failed once again to get up early, so what did it matter anyway?

So, once more, she ended up eating the whole bowl of tuna. With such a full belly, she now didn't feel like doing any press-ups either!

And, once again, she felt the same feelings of guilt about what had just happened.

However, she sought some comfort in the thought that she still had a few days left in which to achieve her goals for the week. Besides, it had been *extra* cold today and no one in their right mind would have wanted to get up early in that sort of weather!

This thought made her feel much better.

The next day she awoke to yet another cold morning.

And once again, the same thing happened.

I really will get up tomorrow, she thought as she settled back down into the blissful warmth of her basket.

This time she didn't even have the energy to feel guilty about it either!

When she finally got up she didn't hesitate to go straight over to her bowl of food and scoff the whole lot in one go.

Once again, the guilt was still there, but it didn't stick in her throat like it had the day before.

The next morning she didn't even bother to check what the weather was like.

She reasoned that the week was very nearly over so what was the point in starting to work on her goals now? After all, it would be best to start afresh when everything was just right – the weather, her attitude and the day of the week. Of course, starting at the beginning of the week was always better than starting at the end of the week!

Yes, she might as well make a fresh start at the beginning of the week.

She was sure that everything would be perfect on Monday.

Once she had made this decision, she immediately began to forget about visualising her goal or looking at her action plan each morning. In fact, by the end of the week she had almost given up on her goal of getting to the Dairy altogether.

Her basket had started to feel much more comfortable again and her bowl of tuna somehow tasted sweeter too.

When the week had finished and it was time to see Polly again, Serendipity was in the middle of a mid-morning nap. She awoke with a start when she heard the familiar whistle from next door signalling that the coast was now clear.

However, Serendipity didn't really want to see Polly right at that moment.

She just couldn't face it.

What on earth would she say to her about her failure to achieve the goals she had set for herself that week?

Yet, once again, the whistle came.

And once again the whistle was ignored.

When she heard it for the third time it started to dawn on Serendipity that maybe she really should just go and face the music. She might as well just get it over and done with now rather than having to explain to Polly later on why she hadn't come when she had called.

So, with her tail between her legs, Serendipity slowly

ambled towards the study where Polly was sitting proudly on her perch.

'Morning Serendipity!' Polly said brightly. 'I was starting to wonder what had happened to you! So, how did you get on with your actions for this week?'

Serendipity squirmed a little before replying tentatively, 'Well, I *started* well by putting together my action plan for the next six weeks!'

'Well done, Serendipity!' Polly replied cheerily. 'Tell me all about it.'

So Serendipity outlined her action plan for Polly.

When she had finished Polly look impressed. 'Well done, Serendipity. So, how do you feel about the actions and the timeframes?'

'Well,' she replied confidently, 'I feel they are realistic but at the same time challenging enough to get me really excited! My success with writing my action plan gave me confidence to start my new diet and exercise regime ... but ... ' Serendipity paused and looked down at the floor.

'Yes, but what?' asked Polly patiently.

'Then, I let myself down by not getting up early in the morning as I had planned.'

'And how did that make you feel?'

Serendipity fidgeted awkwardly for a few moments before replying in a low whisper, 'Dreadful. I felt like a failure. I felt I had let myself down and wondered what was the point in going on with my plans. I convinced myself I would succeed the next day, but it just kept happening again and again. In the end I lost all confidence in my ability to achieve my goal. I actually stopped visualising my goal and even stopped looking at my action plan or visualising my journey. I'm now starting to question whether I will ever be able to get to where I want to be. In fact, my basket is starting to feel quite comfortable again. Maybe I should just leave things as they are and forget about the Dairy.'

She then looked down at the ground and shook her head.

'Right,' said Polly sounding in determined mood. 'What has just happened is a totally normal part of one's journey towards reaching a goal.'

'It is?' asked Serendipity lifting her head, feeling genuinely surprised by what Polly had just revealed.

'Absolutely,' replied Polly. 'You have just come across a particularly nasty character which will nearly always appear whenever goals are set.'

Serendipity was confused. 'But I haven't met anyone this week. I've been alone in my basket all the time!'

'Oh, believe me, you have made its acquaintance and been well and truly seduced by its power. The trouble is, it's so subtle and cunning, you don't even know it's been seducing you!'

'But, who are you talking about? Who has seduced me?' asked Serendipity, getting more confused by the minute.

Polly lowered her head and said in a hushed voice.

'Its name is *Procrastination*. It hates goals of any kind and can sniff one out a mile off. When someone sets a goal, it's drawn to it like a bee to nectar. It then sets out to sabotage the goal by seducing the goal-setter into putting off taking action. It can sense when someone is wavering over taking action and will then seduce them by offering temporary relief from the negative feeling associated with taking that action. However, what it's really doing is offering you a drug in the hope you will get addicted.'

Serendipity was horrified by what she was hearing. 'What drug?' she asked, flabbergasted. 'I don't take drugs!'

Polly sighed, shook her head and replied, 'The drug is called *Inaction*. It will take away the discomfort that is often associated with the thought of taking action. But in reality the relief is only short-lived. When you succumb to Inaction, the discomfort or dread associated with taking action will only come back again, but this time worse than before. Once

Procrastination has you hooked on Inaction, it knows it can come back again and again. In the end you become so demoralised by the effects of Inaction that you abandon your goals all together – and Procrastination is victorious!'

Serendipity was horrified by what she was hearing.

'But, I would never take any drugs – I know they're bad for you!' she replied defiantly.

'Oh, but you didn't realise Inaction was bad for you because it felt so good at the time. That's why Procrastination is so deadly and seductive. Procrastination is masterful at finding your weaknesses and exploiting them for its own gain. It will convince you that you should wait until everything is perfect before you take action. It will offer you a number of reasons why *now* is not the perfect time to take action. Yet, this is a *big* lie. The only perfect time to take action is right *now*. The longer you put things off, the more opportunities will pass you by and the more difficult taking action will become.'

Serendipity groaned. 'I'm already a week behind in my timetable. I can certainly feel I might have lost the opportunity of getting to the Dairy before winter sets in.'

Polly continued. 'Yes, that is exactly what Procrastination wants to happen. In fact, I have spent my life trying to help others to defeat Procrastination. However, it's not an easy task as Procrastination is like a cockroach – resilient and cunning. Whatever you do, never let down your guard, even when you think you have defeated it. You never know when it will pop up again, seemingly unscathed, tempting you once more with Inaction. Only when you have achieved your goal will you know that you have conquered it for good. Well, at least until you set another goal!'

Trying hard to absorb all this new information, Serendipity asked tentatively, 'So, without my realising it, Procrastination came and seduced me, offering me a number of excuses why I shouldn't get up? It then tempted me with Inaction in the form of the comfort of my own basket?'

'Absolutely!' replied Polly triumphantly, waving a wing in the air. 'It will use any resource out there to stop you from taking the necessary action to achieve your goals.'

'So, why do I feel so bad now?' asked Serendipity wearily.

'The effect of the drug is wearing off. You are getting the withdrawal symptoms associated with Inaction – those of disappointment, frustration and apathy!

'You see, Procrastination knows that your brain is programmed to seek pleasure and avoid pain. So, it convinces you that you can avoid pain by succumbing to Inaction. However, as you have discovered, the so-called pleasure associated with Inaction is short-lived and when that pleasure has worn off you are left with long-term pain instead.'

Serendipity listened intently as the parrot continued. 'When you take action, you may have to face some short-term discomfort but you are left with the long-term pleasure associated with achieving your goals! However, the irony is that taking action isn't usually as painful as you thought it would be – in fact it's often rather fun!'

'Wow!' replied Serendipity, absolutely intrigued by these revelations. 'So, what can I do to kick this awful habit of Inaction?'

'The only way to break the habit is to take action – and lots of it! When you reap the rewards of action, you will probably get hooked on that instead – which is great for achieving your goals!'

'That's all very well,' replied Serendipity with concern, 'but how do I make sure that Procrastination doesn't come back and take me unawares again?'

'By calling in a good friend of mine,' replied Polly. 'It knows all Procrastination's little tricks and as a consequence Procrastination is terrified of its power.'

'Who is it?' asked Serendipity, her ears suddenly pricking up.

Polly waved her wing in the air and announced triumphantly, 'Its name is *Motivation*. Once you have made friends with Motivation and felt its power, it will be your friend for life.'

Serendipity was by now completely enthralled by what the parrot was saying. 'So, how do I make its acquaintance?' she enquired.

'Well,' replied Polly, 'Motivation takes on a number of guises. By asking a series of questions, which I call *power questions*, Motivation will appear in the form that is most effective for fighting Procrastination at that particular moment.'

'But, what are the questions?' asked Serendipity, slowly starting to feel more optimistic about beating Procrastination.

'OK then,' Polly replied. 'Let me ask you this: what *will* happen if you *do* get up early?'

Serendipity thought for a moment and then replied, 'If I *do* get up early? Well, for a start, I will feel good about myself and I will feel that I am one step closer to getting to the Dairy.'

As she thought once more about getting to the Dairy and how good it would feel, she was immediately back in touch with the feelings of excitement she had previously felt about her goal.

'So, what *will* happen if you *don't* get up early?' asked Polly.

'That's easy,' Serendipity replied. 'I have already had a taste of that. I will feel disappointed with myself, depressed, and stay exactly where I am. Oh, and I will become hooked on Inaction which will be disastrous! Despite what I said earlier, I *definitely* still want to get to the Dairy.'

Polly nodded, her expression still warm but serious. 'What *won't* happen if you *do* get up early?'

Serendipity took her time to work this one out.

She then replied tentatively, 'I guess I *won't* stay exactly where I am and I *won't* feel depressed. Now I am aware of Procrastination, I *won't* be seduced by it any more and I *won't* get hooked on Inaction.'

Polly nodded gently. 'Lastly, what *won't* happen if you *don't* get up early?'

Serendipity again thought carefully about her reply.

'I *won't* be able to fight Procrastination, I *won't* feel good and I *won't* be taking that first step towards getting to the Dairy,' she replied with a shudder.

'Well done,' said Polly proudly. 'Now, I want you to think carefully about each of these answers. Think about the implications of each and how you would feel about each possible outcome. Then ask yourself which answer would prompt you into taking action and get you out of your basket the quickest.'

As Serendipity thought about each question and how each scenario would make her feel, it became clear to her that two questions stood out like a beacon of light.

'What *will* happen if I *don't* get up and what *won't* happen if I *don't* get up?' she said decisively.

'So Serendipity, why do those stand out for you?' Polly enquired.

On hearing this question, Serendipity felt a lump form in her throat and she replied, 'Because I'm overwhelmed with dread at the thought of Procrastination taking hold once again, getting me hooked on Inaction and then never getting to the Dairy. When I think of these outcomes, I'm so horrified that I could have ever been seduced by this awful thing called Procrastination. I am so against drug taking of any kind. I want to kick the habit right away before it takes hold. Nothing is worth giving up my dreams for, especially not a quick fix like snuggling into a nice warm basket.'

When Serendipity had finished talking, she was instantly filled with a new sense of determination.

'Right, that's settled then,' said Polly. 'Ask these questions whenever you feel Procrastination starting to seduce you. You can then be sure that Motivation will appear and prompt you into taking action. When you have made friends with Motivation, you will be well on your way to conquering Procrastination for good!'

However, despite her new feelings of confidence,

Serendipity was not yet entirely convinced. 'But, what happens if I am *still* seduced by Procrastination? Procrastination sounds so cunning. What if this just isn't enough? Remember, I have felt Procrastination's power first hand,' she said with a shudder. Polly nodded. 'Yes, I do understand how powerful Procrastination can be. However, Motivation has a back-up plan if your power questions fail to deliver.'

'What is it?' asked Serendipity with a renewed sense of urgency.

'You can stop Procrastination in its tracks by creating an anchor,' Polly replied.

'I may feel all at sea and sick as a parrot at the thought of Procrastination,' sighed Serendipity, 'but I don't see what anchors have to do with anything!'

Polly laughed before replying. 'No, it's got nothing to do with ships, believe me! An anchor is a way of pushing a switch in your mind to get you to associate a feeling with a specific action.'

Serendipity was intrigued, 'How do we do that?' she asked excitedly.

Polly nodded. 'OK, what I want you to do is to think of a time when you felt really motivated.'

Serendipity thought for a moment before replying, 'I was motivated when I was a kitten. In fact, I couldn't wait to go out and start playing "chase" with the other kittens.'

'Great!' said Polly. 'Now, I want you to use your new visualisation techniques to create an image in your mind of what was going on at the time when you felt really motivated. Recall what you were seeing, thinking, hearing and feeling. When the experience and the feelings are at their strongest, squeeze your paws together. Repeat this sequence four times, each time adding more good feelings to the experience. Then, while still squeezing your paws together and holding on to those feelings, visualise yourself getting up in the morning and imagine how good it feels to be finally taking action!'

'Sounds great!' Serendipity said excitedly.

'Now, to increase the feelings associated with your anchor you need to say in your mind something like, "I am motivated – go for it!"'

'Why do I need to say that?' asked Serendipity, cocking her head to one side.

'Well, when you use *words* to back up your visualisation of the desired outcome, it serves to further programme your subconscious mind for success. We call this an *affirmation*. When used regularly alongside visualisation, affirmations can be very powerful indeed.'

'So, what other affirmations can I use?' Serendipity enquired.

'Affirmations can be about anything you want them to be,' replied Polly. 'The important thing is that they are short, to the point, stated in the positive and stated in the present.'

'Why do they need to be stated in the present?' asked Serendipity.

'Well, you need to convince your subconscious mind that this is how you are feeling right now. For instance, instead of saying "I really want to feel motivated!" you need to say "I am *now* truly motivated!"'

So, Serendipity did exactly what Polly said. When she had practised the required steps to create her Motivation anchor, she exclaimed, 'Wow! That is amazing! I really do feel motivated now when I think about getting up in the morning!'

'That's great!' replied Polly. 'So, how do you feel now about being able to stand up to Procrastination?'

'Well, I don't think it will be able to pedal its drugs anywhere near me any more, however persuasive it might be!' exclaimed Serendipity triumphantly.

And they both laughed out loud.

When they had finished laughing Polly said, 'Now, there is one more thing you can do to make sure Motivation sticks around after you have made friends with it.'

'What's that?' asked Serendipity eagerly.

'Well, you need to record your progress towards reaching your goals. Every day, you need to make a record of what you have done to take you nearer to your goal. If you do this along with your daily visualisations and affirmations, you will ensure Motivation is always on hand to help you out. The more Motivation becomes a permanent fixture in your life, the more likely you are to attract its best friend along for the ride.'

'Who's its best friend?' asked Serendipity, pricking up her ears.

'It's called *Momentum*,' replied Polly, sitting up and stretching her wings. 'When you have Momentum in your life, Procrastination will probably just give up the fight and leave you alone for good. You see, when Motivation and Momentum work together they are very powerful indeed.'

'Right,' said Serendipity. 'I will make sure I record what I have achieved each day. Hopefully that will be enough to keep hold of Motivation and create Momentum as well!'

'Great!' replied Polly. 'Now, what actions are you going to take this week?'

Serendipity thought carefully before replying.

'OK, firstly I am going to get up at 8 o'clock each day. I am going to ration myself to half a bowl of food, do ten press ups and then I'm going to attempt to get through the cat flap.'

'That sounds great,' said Polly. 'So, when exactly are you going to take these actions?'

'Well,' replied Serendipity, 'I will start getting up early, rationing my food and taking my exercises tomorrow. That will ensure that I start losing weight to allow myself to get through the cat flap. I aim to have lost about 2 lbs by next Saturday, so that's when I will try to get through the cat flap.'

'*Try* to get through the cat flap?' challenged Polly.

'No, *definitely* get through!' laughed Serendipity.

'And what is your level of commitment to these actions?' enquired Polly.

'Well, now I have experienced the power of Procrastination

and its effects, I would say my commitment is 10 out of 10!' replied Serendipity with great determination.

And they both laughed.

On hearing the sound of a car approaching, Serendipity quickly got up off the floor. 'Thanks Polly,' she said. 'I'll get on with these actions straight away!' And she ran out of the door waving her paw in the air.

When she got back to her basket, she made a note of all the things she had learned that day:

* There would be many obstacles on her journey to the Dairy
* One of those obstacles was Procrastination
* Procrastination can get you hooked on Inaction
* Inaction may give you short-term 'pleasure' but leave you with long-term 'pain'
* The thought of taking action may produce some short-term 'pain' but the action will reward you with long-term 'pleasure'
* Long-term 'pleasure' was worth the short-term 'pain'
* Short-term 'pleasure' was not worth the long-term 'pain'
* You can beat Procrastination by finding Motivation
* You can call upon Motivation by asking four Power Questions:
  What *will* happen if you *do* take action?
  What *will* happen if you *don't* take action?
  What *won't* happen if you *do* take action?
  What *won't* happen if you *don't* take action?
* She was most motivated by the thought of *avoiding* long-term 'pain'
* She could also create an anchor which she could switch on when she needed extra Motivation
* She could use affirmations and visualisations to increase her levels of Motivation

- ❧ When you record your successes it helps you to keep hold of Motivation
- ❧ Motivation encourages you to take more action
- ❧ When you take more action you create Momentum
- ❧ Having Momentum prevents Procrastination

She now couldn't wait to put her new skills into practice. She looked at her timetable for getting to the Dairy and realised that last week's inaction had caused her to fall a week behind in her exercise routine. She realised that she would have to work extra hard the following week to make up for this. So, she would just have to start by doing 20 press ups a day instead of 10!

When night fell she felt totally exhausted and looked forward to a good night's sleep.

Yet, a good night's sleep was not what Serendipity got!

That night, her sleep was filled with nightmares. To her horror, she was *not* at the Dairy but still stuck in her old basket.

But this basket was not at all comfortable.

This basket was shrinking before her very eyes, squeezing her so tight that she could hardly breathe. In fact, her basket had now become a prison cell. Iron bars surrounded her and chains shackled her paws. She looked around her, but all she could see was darkness – and a damp chill hung in the air.

8

'Our greatest glory is not in never falling, but in rising every time we fall'[10]

W hen Serendipity awoke the next morning, she was drenched in sweat. Horrified at the content of her dream, she looked down at her basket.

To her surprise there were no longer any bars. With this realisation, she was immediately overcome with relief.

Yet, despite her relief, she couldn't help but notice that the air was still damp and the sky was dark and overcast.

She looked up at the clock and could just about see it was nearly 8 a.m.

Nearly time to get up, she thought.

Yet, it seemed so dark and damp in the room, the thought was not appealing.

She was immediately reminded of how nice and warm her basket was.

'Just five more minutes won't hurt,' she could hear a voice saying inside her head, as she snuggled deeper into her basket.

This instantly made her feel much better and all thoughts of getting out into the cold began to vanish.

And then it hit her.

The voice inside her head was not hers.

She was once again being seduced by Procrastination!

---

[10] Confucius (Chinese philosopher, 551–479 BC).

As she was still feeling a little groggy, she realised she must be an easy target.

She then knew what she needed to do.

So, she began to recall the *power questions* Polly had asked her the day before.

'What *will* happen if I *don't* get out of my basket?' she asked herself.

This question forced her to recall the nightmare she had just experienced. She realised that, if she didn't get out of her basket, she would stay exactly where she was, chained to a life that was no longer fulfilling.

With increasing urgency she then asked herself, 'What *won't* happen if I *don't* get out of my basket?'

The answer that immediately came to mind was *that she would never get to the Dairy and would never get to drink the Cream.*

She then felt something powerful begin to happen.

The thought of staying imprisoned in her basket and never getting to drink the Cream seemed far *worse than the thought of getting out into the cold, dank air.*

So, bracing herself for the cold, she could almost feel a powerful arm lifting her out of her warm basket and on to the chilly, damp floor.

Yet, despite the blast of cold air that greeted her, she hardly even felt the cold at all.

In fact, far from feeling cold, she was instead filled with a warm feeling of pride in what she had just done!

She then knew exactly what had happened.

She had just met Motivation.

This new discovery immediately filled her with a rush of excitement at what she considered to be a great achievement.

Through meeting Motivation, she had conquered Procrastination!

She only hoped that it would remain her friend throughout her long, hard journey to the Dairy.

When she heard her stomach rumble, she realised that the traumatic night had left a big hole in her belly.

She then remembered what Polly had said about rewarding her successes along the way. She looked over at her bowl and saw it was full of food.

So, still flushed with the success of getting up early, she trotted over to the bowl of food and began to eat.

It felt so good wolfing down the tuna that she really didn't want to stop.

In fact, the thought of having to stop was extremely *painful*. 'Just a few more mouthfuls,' the voice inside her said, 'then you can stop.'

Knowing she could have those few more mouthfuls immediately filled her with a warm feeling of relief. Yet, as she saw the food rapidly disappear before her eyes, a horrifying thought occurred.

Was that voice inside her really hers? Maybe she hadn't yet slain Procrastination after all!

Remembering what Polly had said about Procrastination's cunning, she considered that maybe it had just lulled her into a false sense of security!

So, determined to learn from what had happened the day before, Serendipity once again asked herself Polly's power questions.

And, once again she came up with the same answers.

And the answers were enough to stop her in her tracks.

She stared down at the half-eaten bowl, considering how good it felt to fill her tummy with food. So good that the thought of *not* eating the rest of it was very unappealing indeed. In fact, she would even say it was quite painful!

But the thought of not getting to the Dairy was far worse!

This immediately prompted her to turn away from the bowl of food.

Once again, the feeling of pride in her achievement immediately replaced the nagging empty feeling in her stomach. In fact, far from feeling empty, her newly acquired success prompted her to swell up with pride!

She looked at her action plan for the week and knew it was now time to start exercising. Again, the thought of exercising was not at all appealing – in fact it was quite painful. So, before she had a chance to be tempted with Inaction, she began some press-ups.

Although it was hard at first, she still managed to complete all 20 in a row.

Once again she was rewarded with a feeling of pride which stayed with her for the rest of the day.

The pleasure she was now feeling was definitely worth the short-term pain!

Serendipity was so pleased with herself for succeeding in these first two actions that she even managed to catch a mouse! Of course, she took it as far as the cat flap and then let it go – but it was another success to add to her tally today.

She couldn't wait to tell Polly all about her triumphs!

Flushed with the successes of the day, Serendipity remembered what Polly had said about recording her progress. So she wrote down what she had achieved that day and looked forward to adding to that list every day of the week.

The next couple of days continued with similar success, with Serendipity getting up early, restricting herself to half a bowl of tuna and doing her exercises.

Of course, every time she prepared to take action, she felt the familiar voice of Procrastination tempting her with Inaction.

Yet, each time, she used her power questions to call on Motivation to chase Procrastination away.

Although she practised her motivation anchor regularly, she found the power questions so powerful she hadn't yet needed to actually put the anchor to use. However, she knew it might well come in handy at some point, so she made sure her techniques were perfected daily!

So, each day she imagined a time when she felt really

motivated. When the feelings were at their strongest she squeezed her paws together and said to herself, 'I am really motivated – go for it!' While still holding that good feeling and still squeezing her paws together, she then imagined herself getting out of her basket, eating only half a bowl of food and completing her exercises. And it felt amazing!

She then repeated this a few more times to make sure her techniques were perfected.

She made sure she regularly visualised her goal of getting to the Dairy and the steps she would need to take to get her there. She looked at her action plan regularly, recorded her successes and reviewed these each day.

Remembering what Polly had said about the power of affirmations, she decided to write some out and put them where she could see them regularly. As Polly had suggested, she made sure they were short and to the point, stated in the positive and stated in the present tense.

So, to help her with her actions for the week, she decided on the following affirmations:

* I am always motivated and take immediate action
* I get out of my basket with ease
* I exercise with ease and enjoy the process
* I am slim and healthy
* I can get through the cat flap with ease

Saying these affirmations regularly ensured Motivation was always on hand to help out. By taking action, she began to feel Momentum appear as a regular fixture in her life!

As the days passed, Serendipity began to feel there was now far more room in her basket – which could only mean one thing.

There was far less of her!

Could it really mean she had lost some weight?

She knew that the scales were in the room next door which

meant she wouldn't have a chance to go in until her owners went out.

However, she really didn't need scales to tell her that she had made great progress in many other ways that week.

As Saturday grew nearer, Serendipity grew more and more excited by the prospect of finally getting outside – which would take her one step closer to the Dairy.

When Saturday arrived, she had no problem at all getting out of her basket!

She recalled how she had made a commitment to make today the day she would finally get to see the outside world for the first time in two years.

As she looked over at her daily success chart and the number of actions she had completed for each day this week, she was filled with immense pride in what she had already achieved.

In particular, it was now becoming increasingly easy to get out of her basket in the morning, although she had to admit to still feeling a little tempted to eat a whole bowl of food. Yet, she was proud to say that she had managed to resist that temptation every day so far. The 'pain' associated with rationing herself was certainly diminishing day by day. And the 'pleasure' associated with her success was growing more and more powerful.

As she looked at the cat flap and considered the challenge that lay ahead of her today, a thought began to form in her mind.

Maybe she could have a whole bowl today as a treat. After all, she had done so well so far with completing the actions she had set that week. Besides, it was going to be a long day ahead so she would probably need some extra strength and stamina.

Having a full bowl *just* for today couldn't hurt, could it?'

Anyway, she felt confident she had conquered Procrastination for good, and certainly wasn't worried about it returning. She now had Motivation permanently by her side and Momentum was building up fast.

Besides, she always had her motivation anchor to fall back on if the worst came to the worst!

So, before she could change her mind, for the first time in a week, she ate the whole bowl of tuna.

She was immediately reminded how wonderful it felt to have a full belly again and, after all, it was only for today so she didn't feel too guilty.

With her belly now full and feeling in good spirits, she slowly moved towards the cat flap.

As she approached, she could almost smell the fresh air and see the colours of the garden outside.

So, full of anticipation, she began to push her head against the cat flap and felt it move. Excited by what she felt, she pushed a little further.

The flap moved a little more so she pushed again until eventually her whole head was outside.

She didn't dare look to see what was in front of her, just in case she didn't like what she saw. So, with her face positioned towards the ground, she began to follow through with her whole body.

But nothing happened.

Nothing at all.

She pushed and pushed but still nothing.

Help, I'm stuck! she thought, with a rush of fear rapidly flowing through her body.

As the fear built up inside her she began to panic, thrashing wildly in the hope of releasing herself.

Yet, still nothing happened.

She was just about to start crying out for help when a thought suddenly occurred to her.

What will happen if I don't calm down?

What won't happen if I don't calm down?

And then she realised what the answers were.

That she would stay exactly where she was and she would never get to the Dairy.

105

She was absolutely adamant that she didn't want to stay where she was, stuck there in the cat flap.

That would be even worse than being stuck in her old basket!

This thought prompted her to calm down immediately. As soon as she had calmed down, her mind began to clear too.

She then realised that all she had to do was to back out the way she had come. So, she did just that and felt herself slowly retreating back into the conservatory. Although she was relieved not to be stuck any more, she wasn't feeling too good about being back where she had started.

In fact, she could feel a slow depression beginning to form inside her mind with the following realisation:

She had failed to get through the cat flap.

She then remembered she had also failed to ration her food this morning, and this made her depression worse.

Two failures in a row was not a good start to the day at all.

The feelings of elation and pride she had felt earlier had now completely dissolved, along with her hopes of getting through the cat flap.

Not rationing her food she could somehow justify to herself. However, not being able to get through the cat flap was a monumental blow indeed.

If she couldn't get outside, what hope did she ever have of getting to the Dairy? She then considered that maybe she was never meant to get to the Dairy after all. Maybe she just wasn't cut out for the long journey that lay ahead.

Anyway, what was the point in beating Procrastination if there were so many other obstacles in the way?

After all, she didn't control what was *physically* put in front of her!

The rest of the day passed uneventfully with Serendipity sitting in her basket with a pain slowly forming in the pit of her stomach. She certainly didn't feel like going mousing today. Besides, she had a stomach ache so she didn't feel guilty about this particular inaction.

She would get around to doing it tomorrow.

Yes, she would definitely get around to it tomorrow.

That night Serendipity had no dreams. Just a sense of failure and a steadily growing feeling of disappointment growing in her belly.

The next day, she didn't even bother to get up early, ration her food or do her exercises. Nor did she bother to look at her action plan or do her visualisations or affirmations.

There just didn't seem to be any point.

So, she waited with a mixture of anticipation and dread for the familiar whistle she knew would mean that the coast was now clear.

She didn't have to wait long before Polly called for her. So, with her tail between her legs, Serendipity sloped into the study.

When she entered the study, Polly had her back to Serendipity and appeared to be looking out of the window.

Serendipity was not sure what to say, so merely coughed, hoping Polly would turn round to face her.

Yet, Polly did not appear to notice and continued to look out of the window.

So, Serendipity tried again, this time coughing louder still.

Yet, still no reaction from Polly.

Serendipity was in a dilemma about what to do. Reluctant to disturb Polly from whatever she was looking at or thinking about, she began to consider turning round and going back to her basket.

Perhaps now was not the time to talk to Polly after all.

Yet, as she turned to walk away, she decided that she really should try one more time to get Polly's attention. She really didn't want to have to come back another time as this was the only day she knew her owners would definitely be out. This was certainly not the time to give into Procrastination!

So, she turned round, cleared her throat and said in a cheery voice, 'Hey, Polly, how are you today?!'

Immediately the parrot turned round.

'Hi, Serendipity,' said Polly cheerily. 'Sorry about that. I was just looking out for a window of opportunity. I'm fine thanks! So, how are you today?'

'Well,' stammered Serendipity, feeling slightly perplexed by Polly's statement. 'Not so good I'm afraid.'

'OK, tell me all about what happened this week,' replied Polly with concern, cocking her head to one side.

So, Serendipity began to tell Polly all about her week. She explained how it had started off so well, how Procrastination had tempted her with Inaction and how she had called upon Motivation and taken the appropriate action. She recalled how wonderful she had felt when she had taken action and how proud she was of her achievements. She explained how she had practiced her visualisations and affirmations and how much they had helped. She then recounted how great it had felt to be able to add to her success chart each day and how this had sealed her friendship with Motivation, who had then introduced her to Momentum.

Serendipity then went on to explain how she had rewarded her successes by eating a whole bowl of food, which she had hoped would help her to make the next big step of getting through the cat flap.

However, she hesitated before recalling the final piece of information to Polly.

Polly waited patiently as Serendipity gathered her thoughts together.

When Serendipity was finally ready, she began to confess how she had got stuck in the cat flap and how she had been forced to retreat back to where she had started.

When Serendipity had finished talking, Polly merely nodded and enquired, 'So, how did that make you feel?'

'Awful,' replied Serendipity, feeling a lump beginning to

form in her throat. 'I felt disappointed with myself for failing in my main task. With that failure, I could literally feel my dream of getting to the Dairy slipping away from my grasp. After getting stuck, I didn't really feel like doing anything else at all. I didn't bother to get up early today and I ate a whole bowl of food again. I even gave up on looking at my action plan and doing my visualisations.'

'How did you feel then?' Polly asked patiently.

Serendipity swallowed hard. 'It made me feel even more of a failure. To be honest, I almost didn't come in to see you today as I felt so disappointed with myself.'

'OK,' said Polly, 'I understand how difficult this must be for you. However, please don't worry. What you are going through is a perfectly normal part of anyone's journey to reaching their goal.'

'It is?' Serendipity asked, eyeing up Polly suspiciously.

'Well, yes,' replied Polly. 'You see, Procrastination is not the only obstacle you are going to encounter on your journey to the Dairy as, unfortunately, it doesn't work alone. It has many accomplices who all work together to try to stop you achieving your goals – and you have just met one of them!'

Serendipity was amazed by what she was hearing. 'You mean there are others working with Procrastination?!' she said aghast. 'Which one have I just met?'

Polly looked Serendipity in the eye and said very slowly. 'It is a very powerful enemy of Motivation indeed. Its name is *Dejection*. Unfortunately, it is often known to appear when you take action.'

'I don't understand,' said Serendipity, shaking her head. 'I thought when you took action you achieved your goals.'

'Yes, you are right,' replied Polly. 'Action is indeed vital to achieving your goals. However, things don't always go your way, even when you *do* take action. This is when Dejection pounces and savagely attacks Motivation. You see, Dejection attacks Motivation by making you think that you have failed.

This feeling of failure prevents you from taking further action. In a way, Dejection is even more powerful than Procrastination because it has the power to not only delay you taking action, but to stop you dead in your tracks. It can even convince you that you should abandon your goals altogether or make you believe that you never wanted to achieve them in the first place.'

Serendipity was horrified. 'So, because I didn't get through the cat flap, Dejection pounced on me while I was stuck?'

'Exactly!' replied Polly. 'It's just as cunning as Procrastination – and every bit as deadly.'

'But, what can I do to stop it attacking again?' asked Serendipity with a great sense of urgency.

'You need to call upon another friend of mine. An ally of Motivation. Together they have the power to conquer both Procrastination and Dejection.'

'Who is it?' demanded Serendipity, now with even greater urgency.

Polly raised her wings in the air and said triumphantly, 'Its name is *Resilience*.'

'But, how do I find Resilience?' enquired Serendipity with her paws outstretched.

'Right,' said Polly, once more sounding in determined mood. 'To find Resilience, you first need to change your view of "failure". To do this, you need to be aware that Dejection is in fact a great illusionist. It can make anything seem like a failure if you let it. However, you can conquer Dejection by asking another series of power questions.'

'You mean questions like "Why did I fail?"' asked Serendipity, cocking her head to one side.

Polly shook her head defiantly. 'No, that question will just play into Dejection's hands. You should avoid asking "Why" questions at all costs.'

'Why?' enquired Serendipity, before cringing at the obvious irony of what she had just said.

'Well, when you ask "why?" something went wrong, you are forcing yourself to focus on the problem rather than the solution. Instead of asking "why?", it is far better to ask questions containing the magic word: "What?" '

Serendipity was clearly looking somewhat puzzled by what she was hearing.

So Polly continued, 'Let me explain. The word *why* programmes the brain to search for *blame*. In contrast, the word *what* programmes the brain to search for *solutions*. By asking the right *what* questions, you have the power to conquer dejection.'

'So, *what* are the magic questions?' enquired Serendipity, enthralled by what the parrot was saying. So Polly listed the magic questions for Serendipity.

* 'What's good about what happened?'
* 'What can I learn from what happened?'
* 'What else is good that is happening at the moment?'
* 'What stopped me getting what I want?'
* 'What can I do differently next time?'
* 'What else can I do to make things the way I want them to be?'
* 'What can I do to enjoy the process towards getting what I want?'

'So, these questions will *really* work in conquering Dejection?' Serendipity asked suspiciously.

'Yes, they are guaranteed to do the job!' replied Polly triumphantly. 'You see, when you ask yourself these questions, you are forced to see the opportunities rather than the obstacles in your way. With everything that happens to you in life, there is usually a solution out there – you just need to look in the right place. In every "failure" there is usually a lesson to be found somewhere. Learning these lessons gives you the ability to try again in a different way and to even enjoy the process!'

Serendipity was now excited about the prospect of having

the opportunity to slay another adversary. She realised she would need to ask herself these questions as quickly as possible to prevent Dejection striking again.

However, there was one thing that was still puzzling her. She knew that Dejection had done a good job of damaging her motivation after failing to get through the cat flap. Yet, prior to making its acquaintance, why had she allowed herself to eat a *whole* bowl of food and how come she hadn't felt guilty about it at the time?

So, she put these questions to Polly.

'Oh, that was Procrastination at work again,' Polly replied matter of factly.

Serendipity was confused. 'But I thought I had conquered Procrastination,' she replied. 'I had been rationing my food with ease. No one was seducing me this time. I wasn't hooked on Inaction any more. I ate the whole lot because I *wanted* to and I didn't feel guilty about it either. It was a one off – I was rewarding myself for everything that I had achieved so far. Besides, I needed the food to help me through the task that lay ahead. It was nothing to do with Procrastination. I did it of my own free will.'

Polly listened patiently, gently shaking her head.

'Procrastination is cunning indeed. You see, it managed to disguise itself as Motivation. It convinced you that what you were doing was a reward for your action and that what you were doing was a one off. However, never use inaction as a reward for your previous action. It just gets you hooked again. And, I can't stress this strongly enough – there are *no such things as exceptions*. Once you have lost Momentum you lose your bond with Motivation. And hey presto – you are once again a slave to Procrastination.'

Serendipity was finally starting to realise just how cunning Procrastination was. It seemed it would stop at nothing to prevent her from achieving her goals. There also seemed to be no limit to its resources. However, Serendipity was truly grateful to Polly for making her aware of what Procrastination was capable of and giving her the tools to fight the many obstacles that appeared to lie in her way.

'OK,' said Polly with a smile. 'Now tell me, what are you going to do this week?'

Serendipity thought about her timetable for getting to the Dairy and replied, 'Well, the next time I am faced with Dejection, I will ask the power questions you have given me to allow me to conquer it and find Resilience. I will then renew my friendship with Motivation and have another go at getting out of the cat flap. When I am outside, I will be able to ask someone if they know how to get to the Dairy.'

'That sounds great! So, when are you going to do these things?' asked Polly.

'Well, I'll ask the power questions right away and then have a go at getting through the cat flap first thing tomorrow morning. I've noticed there is a tortoiseshell kitten that comes into our garden on a regular basis about noon, so I'll aim to get outside to talk to her then.'

Looking over at Polly she added confidently, 'And, I feel 100 per cent committed to all of the above!'

And they both laughed out loud.

Before she left the room, she got on the scales and to her relief she had lost a whole pound in weight!

As Serendipity trotted back to the conservatory, she was amazed at how good she now felt. Recalling how depressed she had felt that morning, she was so grateful that she had Polly to guide her along such a perilous journey.

When she had snuggled into her basket, she decided to try out some of the power questions that Polly had given her.

So, she asked herself the following question:

What stopped me getting through the cat flap?

The answer hit her straight away.

113

She had had a full stomach when she had tried to get through! The bowl of tuna she had rewarded herself with had probably contributed to her getting stuck. Maybe she was at the wrong angle too! Perhaps she was looking in the wrong direction or maybe terror had caused her to seize up!

What can I do differently next time?

Well, she could make sure she didn't eat so much for a start. She could try another angle and try looking straight ahead rather than at the ground. She could also try some visualisation techniques to help her relax.

As she thought of more and more solutions to getting out of the cat flap, she could feel her friend Motivation starting to return to her side. So, seizing the moment, she asked some more questions.

What's good about what happened?

Well, she had learned how to conquer Dejection. This had definitely made her stronger and she had now discovered Resilience! She had also become much more aware of Procrastination's cunning and its many guises.

What else is good that is happening at the moment?

Well, for a start, she had managed to get up early, ration her food, do some exercises and lose some weight. She knew she needed to record these successes and then celebrate them in order to build Momentum.

How can I enjoy the process of getting to where I want to be?

Well, she could see her journey as a challenge and an opportunity to grow. In fact, she could see it as a real adventure indeed!

As she settled down for the night, she wrote down her successes and made a note of what she had learned that day:

- Even when you take action you can sometimes meet Dejection
- Dejection kills Motivation and makes you susceptible to Procrastination
- Beware of Procrastination disguised as Motivation
- Never reward action with Inaction
- Never be tempted by exceptions
- Exceptions kill Momentum
- You beat Dejection by finding Resilience
- You find Resilience by asking solution-focused 'What?' questions (and avoiding blame-seeking 'Why?' questions)
- These answers bring back Motivation

That night Serendipity slept well, dreaming of a light at the end of a tunnel. The light was pulling her towards a place where the sun always shone and her belly was always at least three-quarters full of cream.

9

'Courage is resistance to fear, mastery of fear — not absence of fear'[11]

When Serendipity awoke from a blissful sleep, she had no problem getting out of her basket, rationing her food and doing her exercises.

She had called upon Motivation by asking the appropriate power questions and she also used her well-practised motivation anchor to ensure maximum protection from Procrastination!

It had worked brilliantly as she pushed her paws together to re-create the wonderful feelings of motivation that she had experienced as a kitten – and then transferred those feelings to the required actions of getting out of her bed and doing her exercises.

She then did her daily task of visualising her arrival at the Dairy and the actions she would take to get there. As she looked at her timetable and action plan she knew that today was the day she would need to get through the cat flap.

She looked over at the door. She then recalled the things she had already done that would maximise her chances of success this time:

1. She had already visualised herself sliding effortlessly through the cat flap and imagined a wonderful world

[11] Mark Twain (American writer 1835–1910).

outside. She knew she just had to keep these images in her mind as she pushed her way through.

2. She had today rationed her food to only a quarter of a bowl and could already feel that her belly was considerably smaller than it had been the day before.
3. She knew she needed to try some different angles to find out which was the best way to get through.
4. She needed to keep her head up and look straight ahead instead of looking down at the ground.
5. She also needed to stay calm.

When she had gone through this list, she cautiously approached the cat flap and began to push her way through, keeping her head held high and looking towards where she wanted to go.

At first, she encountered some resistance and with it the familiar feelings of panic. Yet, despite these feelings, she took a deep breath, moved back a little and changed the angle slightly.

This seemed to break the resistance and she could feel herself moving forward once more.

Yet, just as she thought she was making good progress, she again felt stuck.

Determined not to give in to Dejection, she took in another deep breath and moved the angle of her body slightly.

She felt herself moving forward once more and, before she could take in what was happening, she found herself lying prostrate on the ground.

When she had regained her bearings it became clear to her what had happened.

She was on the other side of the door.

And what Serendipity saw wasn't scary at all!
In fact, it was the most wonderful sight she had ever seen.
She saw green grass, delicate flowers and rows of exotic

looking trees, their colourful leaves announcing the onset of autumn.

The smell was wonderful too. So fresh, so sweet, so clean . . . and . . . she heard sounds that she hadn't heard for years. She heard the buzzing of bees, the chirping of birds and the sound of a gentle breeze blowing through leaves.

But best of all she could clearly see fields and hills and . . . from behind the furthest hill, she saw smoke climbing from . . . could it be . . . yes . . . she was sure it must be . . . *the Dairy*!

Serendipity couldn't believe she had denied herself this wonderful experience for so long. All that time stuck in her old basket, held back by her reluctance to move away from her well-established comfort zone.

Seeing her goal now so clearly with her own two eyes, she realised she had just taken an enormous step towards getting to where she wanted to be.

She now just needed to find directions to get her there.

She knew that the kitten from next door often came over the fence into her garden about this time. If she just waited, she was sure she would appear soon.

Serendipity didn't have to wait long.

Just at that moment, as if on cue, the kitten appeared, sniffing the air and looking cautiously around.

Serendipity was just about to approach her when she felt a strange feeling moving up her body.

She wasn't totally sure what it was – but it caused her to stop dead in her tracks. In fact, what she felt was so strong that, far from walking over to the kitten, she felt compelled to dive into the nearest bush in order to avoid her altogether.

As Serendipity cowered in the bush, she saw the kitten stop to lick herself, before trotting off in the opposite direction.

Serendipity waited anxiously behind the bush wondering what to do. When she was sure that the kitten wasn't going to come back, she felt a surge of relief. She then made her way back through the cat flap as quickly as she could.

Once she was safely back on the other side of the door, she considered what a lucky escape she had just had.

However, once the initial relief had worn off, it was replaced with the now familiar feeling of Dejection.

This feeling stayed with her the rest of the day.

That night, as she lay in her basket, she reviewed the events of the day.

First of all, she had been really proud of herself for getting up early, rationing her food, doing her exercises and then getting herself through the cat flap.

She knew these were wonderful achievements and she made sure she recorded them on her daily progress chart.

However, despite these achievements, she couldn't get rid of the nagging feeling of disappointment caused by her failure to talk to the kitten.

Yet, now she was aware of the power of Dejection, she knew she had to call upon Resilience to stop Procrastination coming back to tempt her with Inaction.

So, she asked herself some questions.

What had stopped her from talking to the kitten?

* She knew she had been held back by a strange feeling – but was not yet sure exactly what this was.

What could she do differently next time?

* Well, she knew she needed to make sure that she spoke to the kitten next time. She also knew that she needed to find out what had stopped her the first time and then find a way of making sure it didn't happen again.

Maybe Polly could help her out with this one? She made a mental note to make sure she asked her the next time they met. So, onto some more questions!

What was good about what had happened?

❧ By 'failing' in a task, she was now more aware of Dejection and this had given her a chance to develop her friendship with Resilience.

What else was good that was happening right now?

❧ Well, she knew that she had achieved a lot that day. So, she would record these successes to make sure she kept hold of her friend Momentum.

When she had asked herself these questions, she immediately felt much better. In fact, an event that had started out as feeling like a 'failure' had ended up seeming like a success! She would even go so far as to say she felt it was an 'opportunity'!

An opportunity to practise her Procrastination and Dejection-busting skills!

It then occurred to her that this realisation was one more success she could record and celebrate that day!

Serendipity was literally buzzing with Motivation and Momentum. She couldn't wait to get up the next day to have another go at talking to the kitten.

However, the next day the same thing happened.

Just as she prepared to talk to the kitten, exactly the same negative feelings began to appear as they had the day before.

This happened the next day and the next.

In fact, by the end of the week, just the thought of talking to the kitten was enough to produce these feelings. Despite her many successes, Serendipity could see that Dejection wasn't going to give in that easily! So much so that she was very grateful when the time came for her to talk to Polly once again. However, as she entered the study she could see something sitting on the floor of the cage.

But she was sure it wasn't Polly.

Firstly, this thing was shaped like a ball and, although it appeared to have feathers, it was a dull shade of grey . . . not the vibrant colours of a parrot . . . and it looked very scary indeed!

Serendipity was suddenly filled with a sense of confusion and panic.

Where was Polly?

Feeling helpless, she looked desperately round the room in the hope of finding Polly.

She then heard a voice coming from inside the cage.

'Hi there! So, how did it go this week?'

Spinning round, Serendipity was amazed to see Polly sitting on her perch spreading her wings, obviously enjoying the sun that was pouring in through the window.

'Where did you go and what was that in your cage?' Serendipity stammered.

Polly merely replied, 'Perception is not always reality my dear Serendipity! Perception is not always reality.'

As Serendipity pondered yet another of the parrot's many riddles, Polly added matter-of-factly, 'So, once again I ask you, how did it go this week?'

Serendipity hesitated before replying, 'Well, good and bad, I suppose.'

'OK,' said Polly, 'Tell me all about what was good.'

So Serendipity began to recall her successes. She told how she had succeeded in getting up early, rationing her food, exercising, losing weight and getting through the cat flap. She then outlined how she had recorded her successes and celebrated her achievements – and how this had produced Motivation and its right-hand man, Momentum.

'That's fantastic!' exclaimed Polly shaking her tail feathers. 'Please, tell me more.'

Yet, Serendipity could feel her mood begin to darken as she then went on to explain how she had seen the kitten but failed to talk to her, not once, but every day that week.

She recalled how she had again encountered Dejection but, determined not to give in to its destructive powers, had called upon Resilience by asking some power questions ... and how the answers had encouraged her to see what had happened in a positive rather than a negative light.

'The trouble is,' Serendipity added, 'despite all my achievements this week, I still don't seem to be able to talk to the kitten. I'm starting to worry as I can feel Dejection beginning to creep up on me again, despite asking my power questions.'

Polly nodded and smiled sympathetically. 'Don't worry Serendipity,' she said. 'That's what I'm here for. Now let me ask you this. What stopped you talking to the kitten?'

'That's just the thing,' Serendipity replied, dislodging a flea from her collar. 'I've asked myself the same question many times, but I'm still not sure what the answer is.'

'My dear Serendipity,' replied Polly, ruffling her feathers, 'The questions we ask reflect the answers we know!'

'What does that mean?' enquired Serendipity, scratching behind her ear, aware that the flea was still at large.

'All will be revealed,' replied Polly with a wink. 'Just start by telling me how you felt when you were just about to talk to the kitten.'

So, Serendipity began to explain how she had felt.

She told of the cold sweat breaking out and collecting under her fur, the lump forming in her throat and the butterflies forming in the pit of her stomach.

When Serendipity had finished talking, Polly gave her a knowing nod.

'Right, I know exactly what is stopping you,' she said in a sympathetic voice.

'What is it?!' enquired Serendipity, scratching furiously behind her ear, still not free of this particularly tenacious flea.

'Well,' said Polly. 'It's probably the most deadly obstacle you will ever meet on your journey to reaching your goal. In fact, it can be far more deadly even than Procrastination or Dejection. After all, they're best friends and often work together.'

Serendipity was stunned. How could anything be more deadly than Procrastination or Dejection?

'What is it, what is it?' demanded Serendipity with increasing urgency, still unable to relieve the itch rapidly spreading from behind her ear to the back of her neck.

Polly took in a deep breath before replying in a hushed voice. 'It's called *Fear*.'

Serendipity was horrified by what she was hearing, yet relieved to now know what was behind the strange feeling stopping her from talking to the kitten.

'So,' she replied with indignation, 'If it's *so* deadly, then how come you didn't tell me about it before?'

Polly sighed. 'Well, there was no point in saying anything about Fear before you actually met it. After all, there was no guarantee you would meet it anyway. Sometimes it doesn't bother to turn up at all, preferring to let Procrastination and Dejection do its dirty work. However, as you seem to be doing very well at beating those two nasty characters, Fear probably decided to put in an appearance to help them out and to stop you achieving your goal. You see, when someone achieves a goal, Procrastination, Dejection and Fear all know they're defeated. Well, at least until you decide to set some more goals!'

'This is all very well,' said Serendipity shaking her head in frustration, 'but I still don't understand why you didn't at least *warn* me about Fear before!'

124

'Well,' replied Polly, 'warning you of its existence beforehand could actually have hastened its appearance and increased its impact. It would have been like a self-fulfilling prophecy. When you actually go looking for Fear, that's often when it comes knocking.'

Serendipity wasn't at all happy about what she was hearing. 'So, how on earth do I defeat it?' she asked anxiously, with her paws outstretched.

'Well,' said Polly, 'you need to call on another friend of mine.'

'Who is it this time?' enquired Serendipity, now determined to defeat yet another adversary.

Polly waved her wings in the air triumphantly. 'Its name is *Courage!*' she replied in a shrill voice.

Serendipity sighed. 'So, what do I need to do to find Courage?' she asked wearily.

Polly continued to wave her wings in the air with great enthusiasm. 'In order to find Courage, you first need to identify what *exactly* it is you are afraid of.'

Serendipity swallowed hard. 'Well,' she said, still not exactly sure of the answer to Polly's question, 'I *suppose* I'm afraid that . . . err . . . the kitten will . . . well . . . ignore me . . . and . . . she won't like me . . . and . . . I'll make a fool of myself . . . and I'll feel stupid.'

The more Serendipity talked, the more ridiculous the answers seemed to her. In fact, she was now beginning to realise how ridiculous the whole situation with the kitten actually was! How on earth could she be afraid of a kitten that was so much smaller than her?

Polly nodded and said reassuringly, 'To deal with Fear, you have to first understand it and then you need to have some tools to enable you to rise above it and then defeat it.'

'So, what do we do next?' asked Serendipity, keen to find out more.

'Well, when you look at the list outlining what you are afraid of, which of those things has *actually* happened?'

Serendipity felt a little confused by the question so replied, 'Err ... well ... I'm not sure ... '

Seeing Serendipity's confusion, Polly added, 'OK, let me ask you this. Which of the following has actually happened?'

1. The kitten ignoring you when you spoke to her
2. The kitten not liking you
3. You making a fool of yourself
4. Feeling stupid when you spoke to her

When Serendipity went through this list, she could see exactly what Polly meant. 'Well, none I suppose,' she replied cautiously.

'So,' asked Polly, 'if none of these things have actually happened in reality, where exactly *have* they happened?'

Serendipity took her time to think about this question before replying. 'Well, I guess in ... my mind?'

'Exactly!' replied Polly triumphantly. 'You could therefore say that Fear stands for *False Evidence Appearing Real.*'

'So, what you're saying is that Fear is really an illusion?' asked Serendipity tentatively.

'Exactly,' replied Polly. 'An illusion created by your sub-conscious mind which it then projects onto your conscious mind.'

'I *think* I see what you mean,' said Serendipity, although she was not yet entirely convinced.

'So, bearing this in mind, what do you need to do to find Courage and to conquer Fear?' asked Polly.

'Err,' said Serendipity, her fur bristling with anxiety. 'Maybe replace those fearful images with good images?'

'Exactly!' replied Polly, her head bobbing back and forth with excitement. 'Visualisation is not only a good way of creating Motivation, it's also a very powerful tool for conquering Fear. By visualising the desired outcome, your conscious mind projects *good* thoughts back into your subconscious mind, thereby programming you for success. You are then ready to take action. Fear is such good friends with Procrastination and Dejection because they all prevent you taking action. Taking action is the only way to really conquer Fear. In fact, you can use visualisation to create an anchor to find Courage in the same way you did to call upon Motivation.'

Serendipity took her time to recall how effective the Motivation anchor was.

'So, what I need to do is to think of a time when I felt truly confident and then create a vivid image of what was happening at the time . . . what I was seeing, what I was hearing and what I was feeling. When this image and the feelings associated with it are at their strongest, I need to push my paws together. I should do this a few times to build up the association of the confident feeling with the action of pushing my paws together. Then, while keeping hold of these good feelings and with my paws still pushed together I need to imagine what I would like to happen when I talk to the kitten – and this will create my confidence anchor! I need to do this regularly to build up the association of the confident feeling with the desired action, and then I will be able to switch on my confidence anchor whenever I need confidence!'

Polly seemed impressed. 'Well done!' she said clapping her wings together. 'Well remembered indeed! Now, tell me a time when you felt most confident.'

Serendipity thought carefully before replying. When was there a time she had felt truly confident?

'Well,' she replied, after much thought, 'I remember feeling confident when I was a kitten. I used to help the other kittens to catch mice as I knew this was something I was good at back then. Helping the kittens made me feel warm, calm and centred. I would definitely say that is what feeling confident means to me.'

'Great!' exclaimed Polly. 'Now tell me this. What would you like to happen when you talk to the kitten from next door?'

Serendipity took her time to think about what she would like to happen. 'Well, I would like her to look up at me with a smile and say "Hi there!" I would then ask her to share some of my tuna with me.'

'And what would she do then?'

'She would say "Yes please!" and we would share the tuna together. She would then purr loudly and we would start talking about the Dairy and how we could get there together!'

'Great!' enthused Polly. 'And how will you feel when this is happens?'

Serendipity thought carefully about how this would feel.

'Well, I would feel ... err ... I would feel great ... I would feel amazing, feel wonderful, well ... err ... warm, calm and confident!'

'OK,'said Polly. 'Now, I want you to practise creating your confidence anchor on a regular basis so you can switch it on whenever you need to create that feeling of confidence.'

'Sounds good to me!' replied Serendipity excitedly.

'Now,' said Polly, 'in order to increase the feelings associated with your anchor you need to add an affirmation.'

'Why do I need to do that?' asked Serendipity.

'Well, remember what I told you about using *words* to back up your visualisation of the desired outcome and how it serves to further programme your subconscious mind for success?'

'Yes, yes I do!' replied Serendipity, recalling how helpful she had found saying affirmations.

She then began to visualise exactly what she wanted to happen when she talked to the kitten. When she had the image clearly in her mind and felt truly confident, she said to herself, *'I am calm and confident!'*

When Serendipity had finished speaking, Polly enquired, 'So, how did that feel?'

'Wow,' replied Serendipity, shaking her head in disbelief. 'It felt *fantastic*! It felt so real in my mind and, when I said the affirmation, I really *did* feel calm and confident!'

'Well, that's the general idea,' replied Polly, ruffling her feathers. 'The more you practise this technique, the more control you will have over your mind and also your feelings.'

'Yes ... but,' stammered Serendipity, 'it's all very well doing this stuff here with you now, but what if I'm *still* scared when it comes to actually going through with it for real?'

'Well,' replied Polly, 'the truth is, Fear never really goes away for good. There will always be new situations you will have to face, new things you will need to try which will cause you to feel scared. So, when Fear takes hold, you just have to rise above it and make your Courage *bigger* than your Fear.'

'But how do I do that?' enquired Serendipity.

'Well, your ability to make your Courage bigger than your Fear depends a lot on your level of Motivation. Now, remember the four questions we used to call upon Motivation?'

'Yes, I remember those.'

'Well, tell me this. Which of those four questions did you find the most powerful for you?'

Serendipity thought back to earlier that morning when she had used the power questions to get her out of bed. 'Well,' she replied, 'it was "What *will* happen if I *don't* reach my goal?" and "What *won't* happen if I *don't* reach my goal".'

'And what were the answers?'

'That I *will* stay exactly where I am and I *won't* get to the Dairy,' answered Serendipity, shuddering as she spoke.

'And how did those answers make you feel?'

'Well, to be honest, the answers made me feel so bad that they forced me to get out of my basket and get going with my diet and exercise plan.'

'OK, Serendipity,' said Polly, swinging back and forth on her perch. 'Now please remind me – what were you afraid might happen when you talk to the kitten?'

Serendipity thought back to the answers she had initially

given Polly and said, 'That she will not like me, she will ignore me and I will make a fool of myself.'

'So, how likely is it these things will happen?'

'Not very likely as these are scenarios produced by my mind. After all, I now know that Fear stands for False Evidence Appearing Real!'

'So, even if these things *do* happen, what would be worse: these things you have just mentioned *or* you staying where you are and never getting to the Dairy?'

Confronted with these questions, Serendipity shuddered and immediately replied, 'No contest. Not getting to the Dairy and staying where I am. That would be much worse!'

'So then, bearing this in mind, what are you now going to do when faced with Fear?'

'Well, now I have spoken to you I realise that, even if Fear appears, I will just go ahead and talk to the kitten anyway because what I will get if I don't do it is far worse than being rejected by the kitten. So, it is *definitely* worth the risk!'

'Exactly, well done!' said Polly triumphantly. 'Now, remind me of what you are going to do this week.'

'Well,' replied Serendipity. 'I am going to practise my visualisations and my affirmations. I will then talk to the kitten. When she has told me where the Dairy is I can start planning my route. I will also start to put together a diet that is more varied and more healthy.'

'When exactly are you going to do these things?'

Serendipity thought carefully and then said, 'Well, I will do my visualisations and affirmations as soon as I leave the room. The kitten usually arrives around midday, so I will go outside just before then and wait for her to arrive. I will then put together my healthy eating plan after that.'

'That sounds great!' said Polly. 'Well, you've made some really good progress today. Your owners will be back any minute now, so it looks like it's time to say goodbye. Best of luck with your actions for this week. See you later!'

'Thanks Polly!' replied Serendipity and began to trot off back to her basket.

However, before she left, she made sure she weighed herself on the scales and to her delight she found she had lost another pound in weight! This was something else she could add to her daily success chart!

When she had settled back in her basket, Serendipity looked out of the window. Although excited about what she had learned in her session with Polly today, she still felt a little apprehensive about trying out her Fear-busting techniques.

However, determined not to let either herself or Polly down, she spent the next hour visualising herself talking confidently to the kitten and saying the affirmation, 'I am calm and confident!'

To her surprise, she found practising the techniques on her own much easier than she had anticipated. The more she practised the visualisation and affirmation, the more vivid the image became. In fact, the image of success was now so powerful that it drowned out all the previous fearful images.

As she perfected her techniques, Serendipity could really feel her confidence steadily growing. So much so that she was actually starting to feel *excited* about the prospect of testing out her new-found confidence and talking to the kitten!

As midday approached, she looked out the window. As the minutes ticked by, she waited with anticipation for the kitten to arrive.

Just then, out the corner of her eye, she saw the kitten appearing over the fence. Not wanting to waste a moment, Serendipity dashed out through the cat flap to where the kitten was sitting, cleaning her paws.

Serendipity then began to mentally prepare herself to talk to the kitten. Yet, as she took in a deep breath to begin speaking, something unexpected happened.

A tightness developed in her throat and she heard a voice in her head saying, 'What if she ignores you when you speak to her? What if you make a fool of yourself? Are you sure you really want to risk it?!'

Serendipity began to feel like she was on the edge of a cliff, staring into a deep chasm but wanting desperately to get to the other side. Yet, it felt like the voice was pulling her back, reminding her of the fate that would befall her if she jumped.

She then knew it was the voice of Fear. Yet, despite this voice of doom, she knew deep down that staying where she was would be far worse than what might happen if she fell. Besides, if she kept looking towards where she wanted to be, she knew she would make it to the other side.

My Courage is bigger than my Fear, she said to herself, recalling what Polly had told her earlier. So, instead of looking down she forced herself to focus on the other side and, before she could change her mind, leapt off the cliff.

'Hi, I'm Serendipity, pleased to meet you!' she heard the words escaping from her lips.

On hearing these words, the kitten stopped licking itself and slowly, very slowly, it turned round, looked straight at Serendipity and blinked in surprise.

Then the kitten began to grin. 'Wow,' she said. 'I didn't know you could talk! My name's Mischief. Pleased to meet you too! How come you never spoke to me before?'

'Err,' Serendipity stammered, trying to find the right words to explain how she felt. 'Because *you* never spoke to me! I thought you didn't like me so I didn't dare say hello!'

'Well, excuse me for sounding like an echo,' replied Mischief, her grin growing wider by the minute, 'but I didn't think you liked *me*, so I didn't dare say hello to *you*! You always dashed off before I could get a word in. Besides, you looked kind of big and scary, so I thought it best not to hang around too long! I'm small and cute, so I thought there was no chance of me scaring either animals or small children! So what's your excuse?'

Serendipity felt extremely embarrassed by what the kitten had said but, determined to carry on now she had found the courage to start, replied tentatively, 'Well, I wasn't *scared* of you exactly, just scared of you not liking me, I guess!'

'What's the difference?' asked Mischief, cleaning her whiskers nonchalantly.

'Ur, well, I guess I wasn't scared of you *physically*, just scared of you rejecting me,' Serendipity replied, recalling what Polly had explained to her about Fear. 'Yes, I was scared of *Rejection*!' she said with more conviction.

'Man, we're all scared of rejection,' replied Mischief with a swish of her tail. 'Well, how come you aren't scared any more?'

'Oh, but I *was* scared ... very scared, but I made my Courage bigger than my Fear!' Serendipity exclaimed, swelling with pride at what she had just achieved.

As she spoke, she realised that, although the visualisation and affirmations had helped with her confidence, what had finally slain her Fear was the fact that she had taken action – even though she hadn't felt completely ready!

Mischief looked at Serendipity with admiration. 'I could do with a bit of that myself!' she said, twitching her whiskers. 'Scared of my own shadow! Would you believe that I thought you might eat me! But, I guess I was wrong about that as I bet your owners leave plenty of food in your bowl. I don't suppose you would need to eat me as well!'

She then broke out into a fit of giggles as she eyed up Serendipity's still very ample belly.

Yet, now Serendipity had discovered Resilience, she didn't let this comment bother her, so merely replied, 'Well, talking of food, I *do* have plenty of food in my bowl. In fact, enough for two, so, would you care to join me in some tuna?'

After a small pause, the kitten shook her head and replied politely, 'Err, thanks for the offer but I think I might pass on that one.'

Looking anxiously over her shoulder she continued. 'Look, it was nice chatting with you but I do have to dash ... see you later!' And with that she darted out of the garden and disappeared from view.

That was strange, thought Serendipity. *One minute she was friendly and the next she was acting like I was some sort of alien. Maybe she didn't like me after all. Maybe she was just putting on some sort of act because she felt sorry for me . . .*

Yet, despite this feeling of rejection, she realised that, even if Mischief *didn't* like her, it didn't actually feel that bad. She was now confident that she could deal with it. After all, the important thing was that she had fought her Fear and talked to Mischief.

Had she *really* felt rejected? Maybe just a little, but she knew she could handle it. However, the overwhelming emotion was one of pride.

With this feeling of pride, something else became clear to Serendipity.

If you leap, you are always one step closer to where you want to be. If you stay still, you will never get to the other side.

Serendipity felt a renewed sense of Motivation appearing and with it was a desire to take some more action.

Yet, despite having found Motivation, as the day wore on, a new emotion began to take hold.

She couldn't get rid of the nagging feeling that Mischief had seemed very strange when she ran off. Come to think of it, she had given her a very odd look and had *really* turned her nose up at the offer of tuna.

In fact, she would even go so far as to say that Mischief had been quite rude!

If she could be that rude, then surely there was no way that she could have liked Serendipity.

If Mischief didn't like her then the other cats might not like her either.

Maybe she just wasn't the sort of cat other cats liked!

It began to dawn on her that, even though she now had the tools to fight Fear, what was the point if no one was going to like her anyway?

To take her mind off these negative thoughts, she spent the rest of the afternoon seeking out mice.

Yet, to add to her disappointment, there didn't seem to be many around that day.

However, determined not to give in to Dejection, Serendipity spent the evening practising her anchors, visualisations and affirmations. She then recorded her numerous successes.

This instantly made her feel much better.

Calling upon Resilience, she decided she would try again tomorrow and maybe take a different approach to talking to Mischief. Or maybe she would find another cat to talk to.

All was not lost!

That evening, Serendipity reviewed what she had learned about Fear:

- Fear will often appear when you attempt something new
- Fear works with Procrastination and Dejection to tempt you with Inaction
- Fear is really an illusion
- Fear stands for 'False Evidence Appearing Real'
- You can conquer Fear by using visualisation and affirmations to programme your mind for success
- You can also conquer Fear by creating a confidence anchor
- You then call upon Courage
- You find Courage by asking some power questions:
  What *will* happen if I *do* take action?
  What *will* happen if I *don't* take action?
  What *won't* happen if I *do* take action?
  What *won't* happen if I *don't* take action?

- You then take action
- Facing up to Fear is less frightening than living with Fear
- Taking action feels good
- Fear retreats when you take action

That night she dreamed about slaying Fear and finding the Courage to continue her journey to the Dairy. Yet, in this dream her hopes were soon shattered when she found that none of the cats liked her when she got there ...

10

'To succeed we must first believe that we can'[12]

When Serendipity awoke, she had the same nagging feelings that she had experienced the night before. Although she knew she should feel proud of what she had achieved yesterday, she still felt bothered by Mischief's apparent rejection.

However, she knew that the best way to conquer these feelings was to face her Fear and take action.

So, she began her day in the usual way by getting out of bed early, eating half her bowl of tuna and exercising. She then looked at her timetable and action plan, visualised herself achieving her goal and then, in her mind, she watched the movie of her journey to the Dairy.

She then imagined herself talking confidently to Mischief and said the affirmation, 'I am calm, confident and liked by every cat I meet.'

She instantly felt better and was now ready to face her Fear.

Yet, when she went outside to look for Mischief, she was nowhere to be seen.

Serendipity waited and waited, but still there was no sign of her.

Refusing to give into Dejection, she decided to try again the following day.

---

[12] Michael Korda (best-selling author).

Yet, the next day there was still no sign of the kitten. In fact, the same thing happened the next day and the next.

By the end of the week, Serendipity was truly convinced that Mischief did indeed dislike her.

What more evidence did she need?

The more she thought about Mischief's behaviour, the more she was distracted from all the achievements she had made since meeting Polly. Her Motivation and Resilience started to disappear before her eyes and Procrastination and Dejection began to overwhelm her once more.

She began to feel down and depressed and was once again drawn towards Inaction, which by now seemed very tempting indeed.

She stopped looking at her action plan and timetable, abandoned her success monitoring chart and no longer bothered with her exercise routine. She even gave up on her daily affirmations and visualisation of the wonderful life she would lead when she got to the Dairy.

After all, if Mischief didn't like her, would any of the other cats like her either? If she was not the sort of cat that other cats liked, then did she really have what it took to get to the Dairy?

She had visualised drinking the cream and knew that it was something she wanted. But when it came down to it, did she really *believe* it was possible she would ever get to drink it?

She knew that she needed to see Polly urgently in order to discuss the doubts that had now formed in her mind.

So, when Saturday approached, she waited patiently for the summons from next door.

When she heard the sound of the car engine outside, she assumed Polly would call her in. However, she heard nothing at all.

Why had Polly not whistled for her? Fear suddenly gripped Serendipity by the fur and a wave of panic shot through her. Maybe something was wrong!

So, fearing the worst, she immediately jumped out of her basket and hurried into the study.

Yet, when she entered the room, Polly was nowhere to be seen.

Serendipity checked under the chair, behind the door and even looked out of the window.

By now, she was overwhelmed with panic. She needed Polly more than ever and just the thought of not getting to talk to her today was enough to send her fur standing up on end!

She was just about to leave the study to look elsewhere when she heard a cheery voice coming from behind her. 'So, how did it go this week?'

When Serendipity heard the voice she spun round and was greeted to the sight of Polly sitting on her perch, happily preening her feathers.

Serendipity was stunned. 'Where did you go?' she stammered incredulously.

'Nowhere, I was here all the time,' replied Polly matter of factly.

'But you weren't in your cage when I came in!' Serendipity exclaimed.

'Yes, I was – you just didn't *believe* I was there! It must have been Fear playing a trick on you!' Polly replied, casually nibbling on a claw.

Once again, Serendipity was stunned. How could she *not* have seen Polly if she had been sitting on her perch? This was extraordinary indeed!

'Well, I was certainly afraid that you had left me,' replied Serendipity anxiously. 'I really need to talk to you urgently.'

Polly nodded and said, 'OK, start by telling me what was good that happened this week.'

So, Serendipity went on to describe how she had used her visualisation and affirmations to prepare herself to talk to Mischief ... and how the voices of Fear had tried to persuade her not to do it ... and how she had called upon Motivation and made her Courage bigger than her Fear ... and how good it had felt when she had taken action and talked to Mischief ... and how positively Mischief had responded.

She then went on to describe how Mischief's behaviour had suddenly changed when Serendipity had offered her the tuna and how Mischief had never returned after that.

Polly listened intently to what Serendipity was saying. 'So, how did you feel after the kitten left?' she asked.

'Well, really rejected,' replied Serendipity. 'I started to think that maybe she didn't like me after all. In fact, I'm starting to believe that the other cats outside won't like me either and I'm just *not* the sort of cat who could ever get to the Dairy and get to drink the Cream!'

'Right,' said Polly resolutely. 'It sounds like you have come across yet another obstacle in your journey.'

Serendipity groaned. 'What is it this time?' she asked, shocked to discover yet *another* obstacle lying in her path to getting to the Dairy.

'It's probably your greatest adversary yet,' replied Polly, her voice tinged with foreboding. 'This character has the potential not only to stop you reaching your goals but to stop you from even dreaming in the first place.'

Serendipity was stunned at the thought of an adversary even more deadly than Procrastination, Dejection or Fear.

'Who is it?' she hissed, shocked at the strength of her feelings of anger and frustration.

Polly moved closer to Serendipity so she was within a hair's breadth of the bars of the cage. She then whispered softly, 'It's called the *Limiting Belief*. It's so powerful, it can literally brainwash you into believing only what it wants you to believe.'

'But, surely you either believe something or you don't!' said Serendipity, confused by this explanation of her new adversary.

Polly continued to explain. 'Well, people often talk about

what they *believe*. But, when you say you believe something –
what do you *actually* mean?'

Serendipity thought about this question before replying
cautiously, 'I just ... *believe* it I guess.'

'Yes,' said Polly patiently, 'but, what makes you believe
something as opposed to *not* believing it?'

'I suppose ... well ... if I think it's true?' replied Serendipity,
not entirely sure if this was the answer that Polly was looking
for.

'But how do you know when something is true?' Polly
continued.

Serendipity carefully considered her reply. On the surface,
this all seemed so obvious – but was it?

'Well, I suppose when I have enough evidence?' she replied
cautiously.

'Yes, but how much evidence would you need in order to
believe something was true?' Polly enquired, her head still
inches from the bars of the cage.

Serendipity could again feel herself struggling for a reply. 'I
suppose it would depend on what it was I believed?' she said, still
not sounding at all sure of the answer.

'OK then,' replied Polly, 'Tell me something you believe.'

Serendipity considered this question carefully before
replying.

'Well, I guess I *believe* I am a cat!'

'Right, so how would you support this belief?' Polly asked.

Serendipity chuckled. 'Well, I've always known I am a cat.'

'Yes, but what real *evidence* do you have that you are a cat?'

'I have been told I am a cat!'

'Yes, what others have told you is one type of evidence. But
what about if you meet another cat – how do you support the
belief that they are a cat too?'

'Well, they would look like a cat!'

'So what does a cat look like?'

Serendipity considered what a dumb question this was. So

she replied confidently, 'Well, it has four legs, a tail, two pointed ears, whiskers, fur, chases mice and purrs!'

'OK,' replied Polly nodding her head. 'What if it only had three legs – would it still be a cat then?'

Serendipity laughed at this thought. 'Yes, of course – a three-legged cat!'

'What if it only had three legs, no tail, one ear, was bald, scared of mice and didn't purr? Would you still believe it was a cat then?'

Serendipity hesitated before replying tentatively, 'Well yes. A strange looking cat maybe – but it would still basically *look* like a cat!'

'But how come it would still look like a cat when it lacks all of the features you just mentioned?'

Serendipity suddenly realised that this task wasn't quite as easy as she had first thought it would be.

'Well, it would still be basically cat-shaped,' she replied, thumping her tail on the floor.

'Ok, then – what about if it was much bigger, say about six feet long.'

Serendipity thought about what this would look like and shook her head confidently. 'No, it wouldn't be a cat then – it would be too big. It would probably be something else.'

'So, what you're saying is, there are certain features or "pieces of evidence" that tick the "cat box". When you have enough ticks it becomes a cat and when there aren't enough ticks, it becomes something else. And some features, such as "size" and "shape" carry more weight of evidence than other features.'

'Yes, I *suppose* that's true,' replied Serendipity, feeling the fog slowly beginning to clear in her mind.

'OK, from what we have discussed, we could therefore think of a "belief" as starting out as a "vague idea". Now, this "vague idea" becomes a "belief" when we are certain enough about it –

and we become certain enough about it when we collect enough *evidence* to support the idea.'

'Err, I *think* I understand what you're saying,' said Serendipity, her tail twitching furiously as she tried to make sense of it all.

'OK,' said Polly. 'I can see you're still not convinced, so I will try to clarify things for you. Now, this principle becomes easier to understand when you have something to visualise. So, let's think of the "vague idea" as being just like the table my cage is on. Then think of the "evidence" as being the legs of the table.'

'Right, that sort of makes sense,' replied Serendipity, still not one hundred per cent sure what Polly was getting at.

'So, tell me this. What would happen if the table only had three legs?'

Serendipity thought for a moment and then replied confidently, 'It probably wouldn't be strong enough to hold you – it would wobble a bit and might even collapse!'

'Exactly!' Polly replied, ruffling her feathers in excitement. 'So, what would I need to do to make the table stronger?'

'Find another leg?' Serendipity offered, thinking the answer perhaps a little too obvious.

'Right again!' replied Polly triumphantly. 'So, when your "idea" has enough "legs" of evidence, then it becomes strong enough to become a "belief"!'

'I see now!' exclaimed Serendipity, beginning to sound much more convinced. 'So Polly, if you are so clear about what a belief is, what beliefs do you have?'

Polly nodded. 'Well, I believe I'm good at helping others to improve their lives. I knew it was vital that I believed this if I was to be successful at what I did. So, I made sure I looked for lots of evidence to support this belief. When I started out, I had no evidence this was true, only *a vague idea* about it. However, over the years, I've collected so much evidence that it has now become a strong belief.'

143

'What sort of evidence have you collected then?' Serendipity asked, now intrigued by the concept of beliefs.

'Well, I know I have helped many others to achieve their goals, and they have shown me much gratitude and thanks and given me lots of compliments too. So, I can safely say that this table is pretty strong! But you know, just finding evidence is not enough to make the table strong. You have to actively collect it and then *fix* the legs securely to the table. You'd be surprised how many people overlook or even throw away good evidence.'

'OK,' replied Serendipity. 'So, what is a "limiting belief"?'

'Excellent question!' replied Polly, looking impressed. 'The example I just gave was an example of a helpful belief, or what we call in the trade an "expanding belief". However, a "limiting belief" is a belief that is not helpful to achieving your goals. Humans in particular are prone to collecting evidence only to support "limiting beliefs" due to a part of their brain which causes them to concentrate on the negative and to overlook the positive! You see, left to its own devices, the human brain can be very destructive! So, humans need to be especially careful to *actively* look for positive evidence instead of the negative stuff.'

'I think I understand now,' said Serendipity, intrigued by what Polly was saying. 'So, what happens once you believe something? Will you always believe it and will the belief remain strong?'

'Well,' replied Polly, 'beliefs are actually very hard to change once they're established, especially in the human mind. In fact, humans will go to *great* lengths to defend their beliefs. When a belief is established, their brains will actively seek evidence to support it, but *filter out* any evidence that may contradict that belief. Wars are even fought in defence of hard-held beliefs! Yet, the really interesting thing about beliefs is that most of them can usually be supported or refuted – you just pick out the appropriate evidence.'

Serendipity felt suddenly overwhelmed. 'OK,' she replied

wearily. 'If you truly *believe* that any belief can be supported or refuted – give me some *evidence!*'

'OK,' replied Polly. 'Let's say that you held the belief that all humans were basically bad and were out to get you. If that is what you truly wanted to believe, you could probably find plenty of evidence to support that belief. You would then just need to focus on the evidence that supported this belief and ignore evidence that refuted it. However, on the other hand, if you wanted to believe that all humans were basically good and would go out of their way to help you, then you could probably find plenty of evidence to support that belief as well!'

When she thought through what Polly had said, Serendipity could see that she did indeed have a point.

Polly continued. 'You see, in order to build a new belief, you have to really *want* to believe it. You then have to actively look for the evidence to support it. It's not always an easy task – but it is possible! You just have to want it enough!'

Serendipity considered her response. 'OK then, if we go back to the analogy of the table representing a belief, then I suppose using visualisation and affirmations are one way of making the table stronger!'

'Exactly!' exclaimed Polly. 'That will certainly provide your *subconscious* mind with lots of strong evidence. But, if you want to make the table even stronger still, you need to find evidence from *outside* yourself as well, which will give your *conscious* mind something to get excited about too.'

'So how do I do that?' enquired Serendipity.

'By testing out your new beliefs!' exclaimed Polly.

'What new beliefs?' asked Serendipity.

'Well, remember you told me that you were beginning to *believe* that the kitten didn't like you, that you're not the sort of cat that other cats would like and you're not the sort of cat who could get to the Dairy?'

'Yes,' Serendipity responded, unsure where the parrot was going with this.

145

'Well, how helpful are those beliefs in helping you to achieve your goal of getting to the Dairy and drinking the cream?'

Serendipity thought for a moment and then laughed. It seemed so obvious now.

'They're not very helpful at all are they?' she replied, still chuckling to herself.

Polly nodded in agreement. 'Exactly! Like I said, not all beliefs are helpful. That's why they're called *limiting beliefs*. So, it's much more helpful to replace those beliefs with *expanding beliefs!*'

'So, what would be some good beliefs for me to have?' enquired Serendipity.

'Well, you tell me! What beliefs do you think would help you get to the Dairy?'

Serendipity pondered this question for a few moments. 'Well, I suppose some helpful beliefs would be:

* 'Mischief *did* like me
* 'I *am* the sort of cat other cats will like
* 'I *will* be liked by every cat I meet and I *am* the sort of cat who could get to the Dairy!'

Polly clapped her wings with great enthusiasm. 'Excellent, those are *definitely* much more helpful beliefs to have! We now need to do everything we can to strengthen those beliefs so they become rock solid!'

The more evidence she heard, the more excited Serendipity became. 'So, we need to find some evidence to make the table really secure!' she exclaimed.

'Exactly!' replied Polly, looking impressed. 'You've made an excellent start by using affirmations and visualising yourself arriving at the Dairy. The more you do this, the more you will reprogramme your subconscious mind into believing this will happen – and the stronger the belief will become!'

'I'm starting to believe it as you speak!' said Serendipity

excitedly. 'But,' she added with slight trepidation, 'it's one thing *me* believing I'm a friendly cat that other cats will like – but how do I get others to believe it too?'

'Well, the more you believe something, the more you will act the part – and then others are more likely to believe it too!' Polly explained. 'Remember, if you dream it you can believe it. If you believe it then you can achieve it!'

Serendipity laughed. 'Sounds good to me!'

'Right then,' said Polly, 'I'm glad that's settled! So, let's start with the belief you had about Mischief. Earlier, you said that you believed she didn't like you. What evidence do you have to support that belief?'

Serendipity thought back to how she had felt earlier. 'Well, she didn't want to stay to share my tuna and she ran off.'

'OK,' said Polly, 'let's start by looking at what she did when you first spoke to her.'

Serendipity paused for a moment. 'Well, she was very friendly so I thought at first that she must like me!'

'Right,' said Polly. 'Now let's review the evidence shall we:

1. 'She was friendly = she likes you
2. 'She ran off without sharing your tuna = she doesn't like you

'So, which evidence are you going to use to support your belief?'

When Serendipity thought back to what Polly had said about beliefs, she realised that she had only been concentrating on the *negative* evidence and completely dismissing the *positive*.

She also knew that it was far more helpful to believe that Mischief *did* like her rather than believing she *didn't* like her. With this in mind, she was now determined to focus on the positive evidence instead.

When she thought about the positive evidence she realised that, in fact, this was much stronger than the negative evidence.

So she said to Polly, 'You know, I really *want* to believe that Mischief *did* like me so I'm going to look for more evidence to support that belief.'

'So how are you going to do that?'

'Well, I guess the only way to collect more evidence is to talk to her again!'

'Great!' exclaimed Polly. 'Now, we can apply these same principles to the other limiting beliefs you came up with earlier. What were they again?'

'I can't remember what they were,' Serendipity lied.

'OK, not to worry. Let me remind you!' Polly laughed.

So Polly listed the other beliefs Serendipity had come up with earlier.

1. You're *not* the sort of cat other cats will like!
2. You're *not* the sort of cat who could ever get to the Dairy!

Serendipity squirmed uneasily as Polly continued. 'Right, let's start with the belief that you're not the sort of cat that other cats will like.'

'OK!' Serendipity conceded. 'If you must!' and continued to squirm uncomfortably.

'OK, so tell me, what evidence do you have that other cats won't like you?'

Serendipity was momentarily thrown by this question. What evidence did she have indeed that other cats wouldn't like her?

Struggling with the answer she replied tentatively, 'Well, when I used to go outside before I got my comfortable warm basket, I tried to make friends with a group of cats. Yet none of them would talk to me. In fact they all just hissed at me.'

'What, *none* of them talked to you and *all* of them hissed at you?!'

As Serendipity considered her reply, she realised that this

was not in fact *entirely* true. 'Well, I suppose not *all* of them hissed at me.'

The more she thought about this particular incident, the more she realised that this was not in fact true at all.

So, she responded cautiously, 'Come to think of it, *one* of them was actually quite friendly!'

'What did this cat do that was friendly?'

'Well, at the time he said "hi" and then, every so often, he would jump over the fence for a quick chat. But then one day he suddenly stopped coming round, so I assumed he didn't like me any more.'

Polly carefully reviewed what Serendipity had said.

'Well, let's assume for one moment that he *did* still like you. What might have stopped him from coming round?'

Serendipity tried to think back to exactly what had happened at the time. 'Well,' she said, 'I guess his owners *could* have moved or he *might* have had an accident. In which case, he couldn't have come round any more.'

As she spoke, Serendipity now remembered that, at about the same time as the cat had stopped coming round, she had noticed that his owner no longer came round to visit either. At the time, Serendipity had just *assumed* that the cat didn't come round any more because he didn't like her any more. But now she thought about it more carefully, it occurred to her that he might just have had to move house and not had a chance to say goodbye.

The loss of her friend had upset Serendipity so much that the next time a cat came up to her she hissed at them before they could hiss back.

That had been around the time that Serendipity had decided she wouldn't go out any more. She didn't want to risk being rejected again. It was just too painful.

Polly could see the pain in Serendipity's face as she confronted these memories. So she continued, firmly but gently, 'So, Serendipity, when you said that *none* of the cats liked you, that wasn't true, because there was a cat who liked you. Is that right?'

Serendipity replied tentatively, 'Well, yes I suppose so.'

Yet, the more she thought about it, the more she realised there were other times when other cats had liked her.

'Now we're talking about it, when I was a kitten lots of cats liked me.'

'Yes,' said Polly gently, 'I remember you telling me about what fun you had as a kitten. So, what do you think now about your old belief that *you're not the sort of cat other cats will like.*'

Serendipity smiled and replied. 'I don't believe that's true any more. Now I have more evidence, I realise I am *indeed* the sort of cat that other cats will like!'

'Great!' replied Polly. 'Now, what about the belief that you're not the sort of cat who could ever get to the Dairy? What would be a more helpful belief to have?'

Serendipity thought for a moment before replying. 'That I *am* the sort of cat who could get to the Dairy?'

'Exactly!' exclaimed Polly. 'Now, let's look for some evidence to back up this more helpful belief shall we? So, what evidence do you have to support that new belief?'

Serendipity thought for a moment and then replied, 'OK, well firstly, I have achieved a lot since I first met you. For example, I have mastered the tools to overcome Procrastination, Dejection and Fear. I feel really proud of those achievements. I have also lost a lot of weight and managed to get through the cat flap.'

As Serendipity went through her list of achievements, she realised that she might *well* be the sort of cat who could get to where she wanted to be! When she thought back to where she had come from, she realised that she had indeed come a long way in just three weeks.

In fact, if anyone could get to the Dairy, she could!

She was now determined to look for some more evidence to make this belief rock solid.

'So, what actions are you going to take before we next meet?' Polly asked warmly.

Serendipity thought for a moment and then replied, 'Well, I'm going to keep practising my visualisations and affirmations regularly. In fact, I'm now going to include the affirmations "I'm just the sort of cat other cats like" and "I'm the sort of cat who can get to the Dairy with ease!" I will continue to monitor my progress and celebrate my success. I'm also going to talk to Mischief again but this time avoid mentioning tuna! I'm also going to start planning my new more varied diet and begin jogging round the garden.'

'That sounds great,' said Polly with excitement. 'So when exactly are you going to do these things?'

'Well, I'm going to get going with my affirmations as soon as I get back to my basket and I will talk to Mischief tomorrow. I will have a chat with her about getting to the Dairy and even ask her to help me plan my new diet and exercise routine.'

'Great!' exclaimed Polly, 'How committed are you to doing these things?'

'Totally!' Serendipity replied without hesitation. 'And you know, if Mischief still isn't friendly, I know I have the resources to cope. I now believe I am *definitely* the sort of cat that others will like. So, if Mischief doesn't want to talk to me, then I will just have to talk to someone else who *does* want to be friendly!'

Polly gave a whistle of approval. 'Great!' she exclaimed. 'You have made some excellent progress today! I'm really proud of you! It looks like it's nearly time to go, so good luck with everything and I guess I will see you the same time next week!'

'Thanks, you certainly will!' replied Serendipity, feeling much more positive now.

Before she left, she had the satisfaction of getting on the scales and seeing another pound drop off! Something else she could add to her success chart!

So, feeling in good spirits, Serendipity trotted back to her basket and reviewed what she had learned so far today.

151

❖ You can have beliefs about anything: beliefs about others, beliefs about their perception of you, beliefs about yourself, your abilities, and beliefs about the world in general

❖ There are limiting (negative) beliefs and expanding (positive) beliefs

❖ Expanding beliefs will help you to achieve your goals, limiting beliefs will act as obstacles

❖ A 'vague idea' becomes a 'belief' when you collect enough evidence

❖ You can collect evidence from a number of sources: what other people say and do; what you yourself say and do; from the world around you

❖ This evidence is collected through both the subconscious mind and the conscious mind

❖ You can provide your mind with positive evidence by using visualisations and affirmations – and by *consciously* looking for it

❖ Limiting beliefs can trick you into focusing on negative evidence while ignoring positive evidence

❖ You can turn a limiting belief into an expanding belief by *actively* collecting positive evidence

❖ The following expanding beliefs would help her achieve her goal:
  – Mischief did in fact like her
  – She was the sort of cat that other cats would like
  – She was the sort of cat who could get to the Dairy

❖ She already had *some* evidence to support these beliefs. She now just needed a little bit more – and she knew exactly where she would get it . . .

152

11

'For the resolute and determined, there is time and opportunity'[13]

The following day when Serendipity arose, she undertook her usual routine of looking at her action plan and timetable for getting to the Dairy, looking at her success chart, visualising achieving her goal, running the movie of her journey in her mind, saying her affirmations, sticking to her diet and then doing her exercises.

As she looked in the mirror she didn't need the scales to tell her that she had lost a lot of weight since she had first met Polly. As she admired her new trim figure she could literally feel Motivation building up inside her!

In order to build Momentum, she then considered what her goals were for this week.

They were as follows:

❖ Talking to Mischief and finding directions to the Dairy
❖ Planning a new varied diet
❖ Beginning her jogging exercises around the garden

She was aiming to start by jogging 10 laps of the garden per day and then slowly building up to 20 laps per day.

She just hoped that Mischief would appear today as she was determined to test out her new expanding beliefs!

---

[13] Ralph Waldo Emerson (author, poet and philosopher, 1803–1882).

So, to provide some evidence for her subconscious mind, Serendipity began to practise her visualisations. She visualised herself talking confidently to Mischief – but this time taking a slightly different approach.

This time she would *definitely* avoid talking about tuna!

So, Serendipity began to visualise herself walking confidently up to Mischief and saying, 'Hi, how are you today? Would you like to stay and have a chat?' and feeling great as she said it. She then saw Mischief smiling back and replying, 'Yes, that would be great! Thanks Serendipity!'

When Serendipity's feelings of confidence were at their highest, she said to herself, 'I am calm, confident and liked by every cat I meet!'

And it felt so real.

At that moment, as if on cue, Mischief jumped over the fence.

At first, Mischief appeared not to see Serendipity. However, with her feelings of confidence at their highest, Serendipity seized the moment and walked boldly up to her.

Yet, as she was about to speak, she heard a voice saying softly in her ear, 'Don't do it, what if she rejects you again? What if she doesn't talk to you?'

With these words, the familiar feelings of Fear began to rise up from the pit of her stomach.

'I must make my Courage bigger than my Fear,' she said to herself. 'I am calm, confident and liked by every cat I meet.'

She repeated this to herself until she started to drown out the voices of Fear.

She then put her paws together to switch on her confidence anchor. This had the required effect and she immediately felt the Fear start to ebb away.

Then, seizing the moment, she heard herself say out loud, 'Hi Mischief, how are you today?'

Mischief slowly turned towards Serendipity and said with a

smile, 'Hey, Serendipity, I'm fine thanks. Nice to see you again. How are you doing?'

Serendipity was stunned. Mischief was so friendly!

However, still feeling slightly cautious she stammered back, 'Well ... I'm fine too.' Quickly recovering her composure she added, 'Would you like to stay and have a chat?'

Mischief grinned from ear to ear. 'I would love to!' she replied, casually licking her whiskers.

'That's great,' said Serendipity, feeling much more confident now. 'I was wondering if I would see you today. I haven't seen you for a while and you seemed in a bit of a hurry to leave last time you were here!'

Mischief cocked her head, looking a little perplexed. 'Oh,' she said. 'Sorry about that. I didn't mean to be rude. It's just I was in a bit of a hurry to get back before my mother noticed I was gone. She is very over-protective you see! In fact, I've been dying to come to talk to you but, when I told her about your offer of tuna, she wouldn't let me come back. She said I should never accept tuna from strangers! But, now you are no longer a stranger, I'm sure she wouldn't mind me staying for a chat!'

'That's quite a relief,' replied Serendipity, wiping her brow with her paw. 'You see, I really wanted to talk to you about something. It's a sort of secret but, now we're friends, I think it would be OK if I told you!'

'Oh, I love secrets,' said Mischief, twitching her tail with excitement. 'Please tell me more!'

Serendipity took in a deep breath. 'Well, I was wondering if you had ever heard about ... the Dairy.'

When Mischief heard these words, her ears instantly pricked up. 'The Dairy?' she replied sounding awestruck. 'Do you mean *the* Dairy?'

'Well, how many are there?' said Serendipity feeling a little bemused.

'Well, only one I would be interested in!' replied Mischief, eyes as big as saucers. 'Why are you asking about *the Dairy*?'

'Well,' replied Serendipity, holding her breath in anticipation. 'The thing is, my goal is to get there. I have made some really good progress so far to prepare for my journey, but I now just need directions!'

She then went on to outline what she had achieved so far, and Mischief listened intently.

When Serendipity had finished talking, Mischief exclaimed, 'Well, I really admire you for setting yourself such an ambitious goal but, unfortunately, I have no idea how to get there. In fact, I haven't yet heard of anyone who does . . . but that's not to say there aren't other cats out there who *do* know.'

Serendipity sighed, beginning to feel Dejection starting to creep up on her again. However, now she was well aware of her adversary, she knew she must call upon Resilience straight away. While Serendipity pondered the all important power questions that would help her, Mischief began to speak up excitedly. 'You know, although I can't give you directions to the Dairy, I think I can help you out with your preparations.'

'That great!' replied Serendipity eagerly. 'What exactly did you have in mind?'

'Well,' said Mischief, jumping up to catch a fly, 'I could help you with your exercises by being a training buddy. And . . . well . . . I think I might be able to help you obtain that balanced diet you were talking about. After all, eating only tuna day after day can't be good for a cat!' she said with a wink.

'That sounds great,' Serendipity replied, 'but, how exactly can I get a more balanced diet? I can't just ask my owners to stop giving me tuna!'

Mischief grinned. 'Look, I'll show you what I mean. You see, I've been doing some detective work since I've been coming into your garden. Why don't you come and see for yourself? I've made a wonderful discovery!'

'What do you mean?' said Serendipity, thrown by this sudden revelation.

'As I said, come and see for yourself!' laughed the kitten. 'They don't call me Mischief for nothing you know!'

So, Serendipity followed Mischief across the garden and, to her surprise, she saw another cat flap partially hidden behind a bush.

The cat flap appeared to lead to the pantry.

So, intrigued to find out what was on the other side, she followed Mischief through the door.

What she saw when she got there not only amazed her but made her mouth water.

On the floor in front her was a bowl filled with chunks of meat in a delicious looking gravy.

'Wow, where did that come from?' asked Serendipity with glee.

'That? Oh, that's my dinner!' replied Mischief with a wide grin spreading across her face. 'Your owners think I'm so cute and cuddly that they entice me into the pantry with some yummy food! But I've just found a stash of goodies I think they were hoping to keep for later!'

Serendipity could now see that Mischief had managed to open one of the cupboards to reveal what looked like a treasure trove. Yet, on closer inspection, she could see it was full of shiny *packets* of food – a far cry from the dull tins she was used to.

Serendipity couldn't believe her eyes! She could see packets of salmon and liver, chicken and turkey, beef and mackerel, rabbit and kidney, lamb and pork, turkey and ham ... all in a choice of gravy or jelly. Not only that, there was a choice of crunchy food as well, all in an array of mouth-watering flavours!

'I ... I ... don't understand,' stammered Serendipity, fighting back the drool now forming in the corner of her mouth. 'How come they give you all this wonderful food when all I get is boring old chunks of tuna?!'

'Oh, they tried to pull that trick on me too,' grinned

Mischief. 'But I wasn't having any of it! You see, I like a bit of variety in my life, not just boring old tuna!'

'So, what did you do? How come they don't give you tuna any more?'

'Well, you could say I "challenged the tuna"!' she said with a chuckle. 'I just looked at it as though it was something the cat wouldn't dream of dragging in, stuck my head in the air and turned my back on it!'

'And what did they do?!' enquired Serendipity, intrigued by these revelations.

'Well hell, they tried to persuade me to eat the boring old chunks by waving the bowl in front of me and practically force-feeding me. They kept saying things like, "Don't be so fussy, that's all you're getting." But, as soon as I took my pretty self towards that cat flap, they soon changed their tuna ('scuse the pun!). You see, they were more afraid of losing me than I was of losing them. I wasn't afraid to walk away ... and showed them with my actions that I meant business! But *they* didn't want to take that risk, so they came up with the goods and this is what they are: yummy, yummy! I think I'm pretty special, so I deserve the best food a cat can get! Whenever I get bored I just walk away and they give me something else!'

'So, what did I do wrong then!?' enquired Serendipity, feeling suddenly angry at her owners for the years of imposed tuna.

Mischief just shrugged her shoulders. 'I guess you just *accepted* what you had instead of *challenging* what you had. You see, if you don't ask for what you want, you don't get!'

'But I didn't *ask* for tuna!' Serendipity said, still perplexed by what Mischief had just told her.

'No, you didn't *ask* for tuna. But you just took what they gave you and they assumed, by your *actions*, that it was OK to keep giving you tuna. You see Serendipity, if you don't stand up for yourself, your owners will walk all over you!'

Serendipity thought about what Mischief had just said. She

then slowly replied, 'I *think* I know what you mean. In fact . . . you are *definitely right*! I will now go back and put what you say into action.'

'Great!' said Mischief. 'Well, enough talking, let's eat!'

And, for the first time in two years, Serendipity had a taste of something that wasn't tuna.

And, it tasted delicious!

As she savoured the different flavours, Serendipity began to realise this was indeed the first step towards achieving her goal of a more balanced diet.

She knew for sure that eating *only* tuna wasn't that good for her, so this was another important step towards getting strong and fit for her journey to the Dairy!

When they had finished eating, Mischief looked up and, with a twinkle in her eye said, 'Look, I had better go. I need to get back to my own house before my owners start to suspect I come in here for some extra food!'

'Well, if you need to get back then I understand,' replied Serendipity, feeling a rush of disappointment that she had to say goodbye so soon.

However, as Mischief trotted off towards the cat flap, she stopped and said, 'You know, it's such a long time since I had any tuna, do you think I could have a quick taste?'

'Sure, help yourself!' replied Serendipity full of surprise, yet grateful that she still had half a bowl left for Mischief.

With that, they both went to Serendipity's bowl of tuna.

And Mischief ate greedily.

When Mischief had finished, she licked her lips and said, 'You know, that tuna tastes pretty darn good. Thanks for sharing it with me!'

'It's my pleasure,' replied Serendipity, swelling up with pride.

'Well,' said Mischief licking her paws, 'guess I'll see you tomorrow and . . . '

'Yes?' replied Serendipity with great anticipation.

'Thanks for being a friend!'
And off the kitten trotted, out of the cat flap.
Serendipity was once again filled with pride at what she had just achieved.
She just couldn't wait to tell Polly all about it.
The afternoon then went by in a whirl of frantic activity, with Serendipity managing to catch five mice!
When the day was done, she felt exhausted. Yet, as she climbed into her basket to settle down for the night, she once again began to reflect on what she had learned that day:

1. She had called upon Resilience, faced her Fear and tried again to talk to Mischief
2. She had built some new 'expanding beliefs' about herself and about Mischief
3. Taking action today had provided plenty of evidence to make these new beliefs really strong
4. Her actions today had lead to results: more confidence, a new friend and a new healthy and balanced diet
5. Taking action felt good – and it had definitely renewed her friendship with Momentum!

When she thought about how much she had achieved that day, she found it hard to believe that it was less than a month since she had first met Polly.
She then felt a shudder down her spine as she thought back to the life she used to live and the way she used to think. Now she had had a taste of a new exciting life, there was *no way* she could ever go back to living that dull, unfulfilling life again!
Yet, despite her feelings of pride in what she had achieved and her renewed optimism for the future, this was tempered by another feeling.
This other feeling wasn't good and it caused her to question why she had spent the past two years of her precious life stuck in her basket, eating nothing but tuna.

However hard she tried, the feeling wouldn't go away. In fact, it stayed with her until the moment she dropped off to sleep.

The rest of the week went by so quickly. Now she had made friends with Mischief, they both regularly popped into the pantry to help themselves to some healthy food – although Serendipity made sure she carefully counted the calories and always had a balanced diet!

When Serendipity awoke at the end of the week, she looked over to her bowl of tuna and saw for the first time it had been left only *half* full.

She realised with a smile that, through her actions, she had shown her owners that she no longer needed, or wanted, a *whole* bowl of tuna.

Yet, she couldn't help but feel a small twinge of smugness when she thought about the newly-acquired stash of food in the cupboard in the pantry – and the fact that it was now Mischief who ate most of her tuna!

Only a balanced diet would now do for Serendipity!

That night she slept like a log, dreaming of a land where she could eat whatever she wanted – and tuna was banned from the menu!

12

'Forget regret, or life is yours to miss'[14]

When Serendipity awoke, she realised with anticipation that it was time to see Polly once more. Although she was excited at the prospect of telling Polly all about her successes, she was also keen to tell her about the nagging feelings that just wouldn't go away.

Yet, despite these negative feelings, she made sure she went through her usual routine of looking at her timetable and action plan, adding to her daily success chart, doing her visualisations and affirmations, eating healthily and completing her exercises. When she had finished these tasks, she immediately felt better.

She then heard the familiar whistle from next door and looked up at the clock, realising her owners must have made an early trip out today.

Well, the early cat catches the cream! she thought with a smile and rushed next door to see her friend.

When she entered the room, she was surprised to see Polly hanging upside down from her perch.

'What are you doing?' asked Serendipity, amazed by this acrobatic feat.

'Oh, just hanging around,' replied Polly cheerfully and immediately swung round so she was once again sitting upright on her perch.

'Right, glad we got that straightened out,' she said ruffling her feathers. 'Now, tell me all about how you got on this week!'

---

[14] From the musical *RENT* by Jonathan Larson (1961–1996).

'Oh, it was brilliant,' replied Serendipity grinning from ear to ear.

'Great. Please continue,' encouraged Polly, spreading her wings and stretching.

So, Serendipity began to tell Polly all about what had happened with Mischief and how much she had learned from the experience.

'Wow, that's fantastic!' said Polly, hopping onto her swing. 'So, how do you feel about what you have achieved so far?'

Serendipity replied with a huge grin on her face, 'Amazing! I have made a new friend, gained a training buddy and found some new tasty food which will give me the well balanced diet I so desperately need! I even managed to do 20 laps of the garden with Mischief helping me. I have lost loads of weight this week and it feels great! You know, I'm so glad I took the risk and spoke to Mischief again. And you were right ... I was letting Fear provide me with false evidence! I'm so glad you showed me how to find Courage, stand up to Fear and look for evidence to build new expanding beliefs! Although Mischief doesn't know how to get to the Dairy, I still feel an amazing sense of achievement. Yet ... '

Serendipity paused and hung her head, avoiding Polly's gaze.

'What's wrong?' asked Polly, with obvious concern.

'The thing is,' replied Serendipity, 'although I feel so positive about everything I have achieved and am so excited about the future, there's still this nagging feeling that won't go away. I don't know exactly what it is but I keep thinking about all the years I wasted sitting in my basket. These feelings are stopping me enjoying my success. Polly, I keep asking myself, '"Why didn't I do something before?", "Why, did I just sit in my basket day after day watching my life pass me by?" It's really eating me up inside.'

Polly sighed, nodded patiently and replied, 'This is the final adversary you will have to face in your journey. The fact that it has appeared now is a sign of just how far you have indeed come. You see, Procrastination, Dejection, Fear and Limiting Beliefs have all failed to stop you taking action and moving towards your goal. So, they have called upon a trusted friend of theirs, who is their last hope of sabotaging your success.'

Serendipity groaned. 'I don't believe there is *still* something stopping me from achieving my goal of getting to the Dairy and drinking the Cream! Tell me Polly, what is this obstacle and how do I get over it?'

Polly moved closer to the bars of her cage and said softly in Serendipity's ear, 'Its name is *Regret*. It will appear naturally when you succumb to Inaction. However, it often appears even when you *do* take action and its role then is to stop you from enjoying your success. You inadvertently attract it when you ask questions such as "Why didn't I do something before?" or "Why did I put things off for so long?" When you come across Regret, it can often lead you back to Dejection.'

'But, how do I deal with Regret?' asked Serendipity, indeed beginning to feel Dejection creeping up once more.

'Well,' replied Polly. 'First of all you need to call upon Acceptance. You do this by acknowledging that what's done is done and the past can't be changed. Once you have done this you are in a better position to deal with Regret. You then deal with Regret in the same way as you dealt with Dejection.'

'You mean by asking some power questions?' asked Serendipity tentatively.

'Exactly!' replied Polly triumphantly.

She then outlined the questions Serendipity needed to ask to deal with Regret.

* What is good that is happening now?
* What can I learn from what happened in the past?
* How can I use this to make things even better in the future?

165

❧ How can I enjoy the process towards making things better?

Polly then went on to explain, 'By asking these questions, you will begin to realise that, even though you *can't* change what has happened in the past, you *can* use what you have learned to make things better in the future – and to enjoy yourself in the process!'

'Oh!' exclaimed Serendipity. 'Sounds easy! I'm getting quite good at these power questions! I can't believe I didn't think of using them before! I certainly won't let Regret take hold again and spoil my enjoyment of all that I have achieved!'

So, taking Polly's advice, she began to ask herself some questions:

What is good that is happening now?

'Well, I have made lots of progress towards reaching my goal. I have found ways to beat Procrastination, Dejection and Fear. I am pretty much on schedule for getting to the Dairy. I have lost loads of weight, look slim and healthy and, before Regret took hold, I felt really great! I have also made a good friend in Mischief.'

What can I learn from what happened in the past?

'Well, the main thing I have learned is that, if you stay where you are, you will never get to where you want to be. You need to take time to dream, set goals, and then take action. There may be some short-term pain involved in taking action but the long-term pleasure you get from achieving your goals is worth it. The best time to take action is right away!'

How can I use this to make things even better in the future?

'To make sure that I never let Procrastination, Dejection, Fear, Limiting Beliefs or Regret stop me from taking the required action in the future. And, to make sure that I never stop dreaming and I never stop believing!'

How can I enjoy the process towards making things better?

'Well, I can enjoy the journey and see each obstacle as an opportunity to grow! After all, there are no such things as obstacles – only lessons I can learn from!'

When Serendipity had finished asking the power questions, she was aware that the feelings of Regret had miraculously vanished. Instead, there was now a feeling of pride in what she had achieved and excitement for what the future might hold.

Polly let out a low whistle. 'So, tell me Serendipity, how do you feel now?'

When Serendipity had finished outlining to Polly exactly how good she felt, Polly asked her, 'So, what actions are you going to take this week?'

Serendipity once again referred to her timetable for getting to the Dairy.

'Well, the next step is to get across the wall of the garden, ask the other cats if they know how to get to the Dairy and then start recruiting others to join me in my journey.'

Polly bobbed her head in agreement. 'Great, so what are you going to do first?'

'Well, now I'm spending more time in the garden, I'm going to gradually build up the number of laps I can complete. Last week I managed 20 laps a day so I will start to build those up to 30.'

'Great!' exclaimed Polly, waving a wing in the air. 'So, when are you going to start doing this?'

Serendipity cocked her head to one side as she considered her reply. 'Well, not wanting to run into Procrastination again, I will start as soon as I leave this room!'

167

'That sounds great!' replied Polly. 'What about getting over the wall and talking to the other cats? When are you going to do that?'

'I will try to get over the wall next Saturday, which will give me nearly a week to increase my fitness levels before giving it a go!'

'*Try* to get over the wall?!

'No, *definitely* get over the wall!' Serendipity laughed.

'OK,' said Polly, casually swinging from side to side. 'What obstacles might there be to carrying out these actions?'

Serendipity thought carefully before replying. 'Well, I feel I am now in control of Procrastination, Dejection, Limiting Beliefs and Fear. I now know how to deal with Regret, so the only obstacle left will be the weather! But the forecast for this week is good, so I can't think of anything else that will stop me!'

'Sounds fantastic, Serendipity!' Polly exclaimed. 'So, what is your level of commitment to doing all these things?'

'Well,' replied Serendipity with great enthusiasm. 'It's definitely 10 out of 10!'

Although Polly would once have challenged such a high score, Serendipity now knew that Polly trusted her to mean exactly what she said when she talked about her level of commitment!

Finally, before she left, Serendipity checked her weight and was pleased to see she had lost two more pounds!

As Serendipity prepared to leave, Polly unexpectedly let out a huge sigh. 'You know Serendipity, I feel so proud of everything you have achieved so far. In fact, I feel very confident that you will achieve all your actions again this week. So, I wish you good luck and hope to see you the same time next week!'

'See you next week!' exclaimed Serendipity. 'By then I will be fit enough to begin my journey to the Dairy with a whole army of other cats on board!' She then waved her paw and trotted back towards the conservatory.

As Serendipity left the room, she heard a voice calling out behind her.

Filled with curiosity, she went back to the study and saw that Polly had hopped off the swing and was now sitting back on her perch.

'Yes, Polly?' Serendipity enquired, wondering why she had been called back.

This was indeed highly unusual.

'I just wanted to say once more how proud I am of you and all you have achieved. I also wanted you to know that I have total faith in your ability to reach the Dairy.'

Serendipity swallowed, feeling a lump forming in her throat.

'Yes, I do indeed feel confident that I can get to the Dairy,' Serendipity replied. 'But Polly, I still don't feel any nearer to solving the riddle you set me when I first met you. You said when I had discovered the answer to the riddle I would be close to finding the Dairy.'

Serendipity then paused for a moment as she tried desperately to remember the riddle Polly had set her.

Suddenly it came to her.

Knowledge of what is, does not open the door directly to what should be.

'I have to confess, I'm no nearer to understanding what this means. Nor am I any nearer to discovering the meaning of my name,' Serendipity exclaimed with a sigh. She then thought back to what Polly had said about her name when they had first met.

When the time is right, it will become clear to you exactly what your name means and why it was given to you!

Polly smiled and said, 'My dear Serendipity, you are so close

169

to solving more than you think. Now go and get on with your actions for the week!'

'OK, Polly, if you say so!' Serendipity laughed, and trotted off once more towards the door.

Not wanting to waste a moment she sped out of the room, determined to get going on her exercise programme straight away.

What Polly had said about having confidence in her abilities had warmed her heart.

Yet, she remained mystified by Polly's riddles.

Not wishing to ponder too long on these unresolved mysteries, she shot through the cat flap to begin her exercises. She immediately caught sight of Mischief trotting towards her.

'Hi, Serendipity, good to see you in the great outdoors!' Mischief said cheerily. 'What are you up to today?'

'Well, I'm about to get going with my exercise programme!' exclaimed Serendipity excitedly and then outlined to Mischief her aims for the week.

'Let me help you out!' said Mischief with great enthusiasm. 'Let's have a race!'

'Sounds great!' replied Serendipity with glee. 'You're on!'

So, they began running found the garden together, one lap at a time.

By the end of the day Serendipity was exhausted. Yet she felt amazing, knowing she had taken yet another important step towards getting to the Dairy.

That night, she reflected on what she had learned that day:-

* Even when you take action and move towards your goals, you may still come across Regret
* Regret can stop you enjoying your success
* This can lead back to Dejection
* You beat Regret by first calling on Acceptance

You then ask yourself the following power questions:

* What is good that is happening now?
* What can I learn from what has happened in the past?'
* How can I use this to make things even better in the future?
* How can I enjoy the process while working towards making things better?

Furthermore:

* She had exercised hard and managed 30 laps of the garden today
* Despite this feat, she still felt *far more* energised than she had ever done before
* Although Mischief had won every race, Serendipity didn't mind as she knew deep down that the race was really against herself – and in that particular race, she was always a winner

Over the next week, Serendipity continued with her exercise plan, each day managing a further lap of the garden. Mischief continued to encourage her, competing to beat her speeds. Towards the end of the week, Serendipity began to slowly catch up on Mischief, until the time came when she actually won!

Yet, Serendipity knew it didn't really matter who won.

What mattered most was that Serendipity could feel her stamina increasing with every day that passed.

When she caught a glimpse of herself in the mirror, she really couldn't believe that it was only six weeks since she had first met Polly.

Instead of the old, overweight Serendipity with dull, matted fur, she now saw a slim, youthful cat with a glossy black and white coat.

Best of all, she now smelt so fresh that even the fleas seemed to have retreated!

She couldn't believe the transformation brought about by a combination of eating less, having a more balanced diet, getting outside and exercising.

Yet, despite this physical transformation, she realised that the biggest change had been the transformation going on *inside* her. Instead of experiencing lethargy, boredom and apathy she now felt energised, positive and totally confident.

Her world was no longer defined by the four sides of her basket and the familiarity of her routine. Instead, her life had now become an exciting place full of adventures, where she saw opportunities rather than obstacles and lessons learned rather than failures.

At times, she was still tempted by Procrastination, encountered Dejection, Fear, Limiting Beliefs and Regret – but never gave into them. By using her new-found tools, she always managed to take the necessary action to overcome the obstacles that confronted her on a daily basis. In fact, it was becoming clear that the buzz she got from taking action had led her to become addicted to a new powerful drug – and that was action itself!

She felt proud to have made two new friends and was now determined to meet some of the other cats who lived in the lane, make some more friends and find directions to the Dairy.

She now just needed to get over the wall and out of the garden.

The night before she was due to attempt to climb the wall, Serendipity slept like a log. First she dreamed she was a mountaineer, fearlessly scaling the highest mountain in the world. She was then an Olympic swimmer, effortlessly slicing through the water to swim the world's largest river. Finally, she dreamed she was a marathon runner, running towards the Dairy, cheered on by each and every cat that lived in the lane.

13

'Success has always been easy to measure. It is the distance between one's origins and one's final achievement'[15]

When Serendipity awoke, she was immediately filled with excitement, as today was the day she was due to climb the wall! Yet she also felt a small twinge of Fear when she thought about the enormous obstacle that now lay in front of her.

However, she soon found that by visualising herself effortlessly climbing the wall, she was able to build up a strong belief in her ability to get over to the other side. After all, she knew that she had once been a good climber and, thanks to her exercise programme, she was now in excellent physical shape.

What more evidence did she need?

Besides, she knew she now had the tools to cope even if she wasn't able to get over the wall the first time around.

To help strengthen this expanding belief, she came up with the following affirmation.

I am a brilliant climber who can scale the wall with ease!

After saying this a few times, she could literally feel the confidence building up inside her.

From her position on the windowsill she could still see the

---

[15] Michael Korda (best-selling author).

smoke in the distance rising up from behind the furthest hill. She could see that in front of the hill was a large field and in front of the field was a river and in front of the river was the wall she would now need to get over.

She reminded herself that, although the wall might indeed be an obstacle, she needed to look for possible opportunities to help her get over it.

Thinking about the sort of questions she knew Polly would have asked her, she said out loud, 'What can I do to get over that wall?'

Serendipity then let her mind relax as she studied the wall.

She could see it was made of stone and was high enough to once again produce the familiar voice of Fear.

'It's far too high. What if you fall?' the voice whispered softly in her ear.

She immediately felt the familiar feelings rise up within her. A lump formed in her throat and the sweat started to prick the skin beneath her fur.

To combat these feelings, Serendipity thought about the evidence in front of her.

Was this real evidence or false evidence appearing real?! Was the wall really so high or was Fear just playing tricks on her?

There was only one way to find out!

So, Serendipity made her way through the cat flap. She knew she had once been good at climbing. But how good was she now? After all, she hadn't tried to climb anything for well over two years.

She knew that she would need to give it a go because the thought of staying where she was seemed far more frightening now than the height of the wall.

So, taking a deep breath, Serendipity took a leap at the wall and tried to climb it . . . but immediately fell back down with a thud.

OK, that didn't work! she thought.

Determined not to give into Dejection, she asked herself the following question.

What might be stopping me getting over the wall?

Well, to start with, her claws hadn't anything to grab hold of.

What else can I try? How can I do things differently next time?

Find something to grab hold of!
But what exactly?
Serendipity looked around to see what opportunities were available to her. She used all her senses to take in her environment. She could smell something sweet, but what was it?
She looked along the wall to where she thought the smell was coming from. She then saw a plant with beautiful white flowers and delicate green leaves. She was immediately drawn to its beauty and intoxicating scent.
Yet, how could it possibly help her to get to the top of the wall?
She then noticed that it was attached to something.
As she approached the plant, she could see it was growing all the way up the wall. The nearer she got, the more it became clear that the plant was attached to something else.
Yes, it was attached to a wooden trellis that went up the entire length of the wall!
It then struck Serendipity that she could use the trellis to help her climb up!
She felt suddenly excited by this possibility. However, it soon occurred to her that it was no good getting over the wall if there was nothing to help her down the other side.
So, she stood staring at the wall, wondering once again how on earth she could get over this particular obstacle.
Finding no immediate answers, she considered that she

should at least *try* to get to the top and then look for new opportunities the other side.

The thought of climbing such a high wall still filled Serendipity with Fear – yet the thought of getting to the Dairy spurred her on.

So, she took in a deep breath and started to climb the trellis. At first she found it hard going and could feel Fear starting to creep through her body. Yet, making her Courage bigger than her Fear, she kept her eyes focused on where she wanted to go and, before long, she was climbing up with ease.

When she got to the top she was amazed and surprised by what she saw.

Instead of the steep drop that she was expecting, she saw a gently sloping roof, which led to a very small drop indeed!

Realising how easy the descent would now be, Serendipity slid effortlessly down the roof and plopped gently onto the ground.

She was now in the field which led to the river which led to the hill ... which she was sure must lead to the Dairy.

She now just needed to find some cats to give her directions!

Seeing no other cats in the immediate vicinity, she decided she would need to cross the river.

Yet, now she was on the other side of the wall she could see that, far from being a raging river, she was instead looking at a gently flowing stream. However, from where she was standing, it still looked pretty deep!

She had often been told that cats didn't like water, so she didn't really fancy having to swim.

Looking for another way to get across, she saw there was a thin plank making a bridge across the stream. Yet, the thought of having to cross the plank and risk falling into the water once again filled her with Fear.

So, she began to think about her goal of getting to the Dairy. She then thought about what would happen if she didn't get there. The conclusion was that, however scared she was of the water, the thought of staying this side of the stream was far worse!

So, she began tentatively walking towards the plank. Yet, as she approached the plank, something in the corner of her eye forced her to stop in her tracks.

Something was curled up next to the plank!

And it looked exactly like a snake!

How could she get across the stream with a snake in the way?!

However, instead of giving into Fear, she immediately began to think of ways to get around this particular obstacle.

She was pretty sure that snakes didn't eat cats. Not completely sure, but pretty sure! Besides, the snake looked like it was sleeping so, if she was quiet, maybe it would *stay* sleeping.

As Serendipity slowly approached the snake, it became clear that what was curled up by the plank was not in fact sleeping.

In fact, it wasn't even breathing!

In fact, it wasn't a snake at all! It was just a coil of rope!

When Serendipity realised what it was she burst out laughing.

Her Fear had definitely been playing tricks on her!

So, confidently passing by the rope she then cautiously stepped onto the plank, testing its strength. Despite a slight wobble, she was determined not to let that put her off crossing the stream. Once again, she felt Fear rise up within her. And, once again, Serendipity made her Courage bigger than her Fear and kept her eyes firmly focused on where she wanted to go.

And where she wanted to go was on the other side!

So, despite a few more wobbles, she managed to safely cross to the other side. Yet again, Serendipity felt so proud of herself for conquering her Fear. She then looked ahead and could see the hill in the distance. Yet, somehow it looked different now she was on the other side of the stream.

Was the hill really so far away or was it just ... small?

As Serendipity made her way towards the hill, it soon became clear that, in fact, this was not a field at all. It was more like ... *a lawn* ... and what had looked from a distance like hills were in fact just piles of leaves that had been swept up by the gardener.

Stopping to take in the scent of fallen autumn leaves, she looked up and saw that the sky was now a deep azure blue.

How free she now felt, standing here in the open air, with the Dairy getting closer by the minute.

With the furthest hill in her sights, Serendipity started to move faster now. Yet, the closer she got, the more it became clear that what she was aiming for was not a hill either.

In fact, it was nothing more than a mound of compost! It had just *looked* like the furthest hill from her basket in the window.

Yes, it had looked like a big hill far away, when in reality it was just a small mound close by!

Thinking how wrong she had been about the height of the wall, the size of the river, the field and the hill, Serendipity was immediately reminded of something Polly had often said.

Perception is not always reality my dear Serendipity. Perception is not always reality!

So, realising that she no longer had a steep hill to climb, she began to tentatively walk around the mound.

When she got to the other side, to her surprise she saw a gently rising swirl of smoke coming from, not a chimney, but what looked like a pile of leaves slowly smouldering in a heap.

And sitting around the leaves was a group of cats!

And some of these cats looked very familiar!

There was Ginger, Tabby, Snowy, Smudge, plus a host of other cats she had never seen before.

The cats all turned to look at Serendipity.

'Who are you?' one of them enquired, eyeing her up suspiciously.

'Err, my name's Serendipity,' she replied, feeling a little overwhelmed by the sudden attention.

On hearing her name, the cats all looked at each other incredulously.

'Not *the* Serendipity?' asked Ginger with excitement.

Serendipity was thrown by this question. 'Err, how many of us are there?' she replied tentatively.

'Only the one, I gather,' said Ginger cheerily. 'It is such an honour to meet you. We have all heard about your many adventures.'

Serendipity was now even more confused. 'Err, what have you heard?' she asked, scratching nervously behind her ear.

Tabby then interjected. 'We have heard that you are a cat of great strength and courage, that you have travelled a long, long way to get here and fought many adversaries along the way!'

'Yes!' added Snowy. 'We heard how you have fought many monsters, braved raging rivers and scaled mountains of great height!'

Serendipity listened in amazement to what the cats were saying about her. It sounded so impressive she didn't have the heart to tell them that, far from travelling a great distance, she had in fact only come from next door!

'Err, how do you know about all this?' asked Serendipity, intrigued to find out more.

'Oh, a little bird told us,' replied Smudge with a wink.

Before Serendipity had a chance to open her mouth, another cat spoke up.

'What prompted you to travel so far and brave such adversities?' the cat enquired wide eyed with admiration.

Serendipity bit her lip, not exactly sure how to reply to this particular question. However, she soon came to the conclusion that, as she had come this far, she had better cut to the chase.

'Well, err, I'm on my way to find the Dairy,' she stammered. 'I don't suppose any of you know how to get there?'

Once again, the cats all looked at each other, shaking their heads in amazement.

Eventually an elderly grey cat spoke up. She sighed and said gently, 'We're all searching for the Dairy, my dear. Trouble is, no one knows where it is. Generation after generation have been searching for it, but no one has found it yet – or if they have, they certainly haven't told anyone else!'

'I think it's just a rural myth myself,' interjected Ginger. 'Sounds like a scam to me. Can't see how all your dreams can come true just from drinking some old cream!'

'I think it's a lovely story,' said Snowy as she sat up and yawned. 'It's nice to believe in something like the Dairy. It's a story of hope you can pass on to your children and the next generation after that. It's nice to be able to dream that one day you might find the Dairy and all your dreams will come true!'

Serendipity's heart sank. She felt a wave of disappointment overwhelm her as she felt her goal rapidly slipping away from her. If none of these cats knew where the Dairy was, then what hope did she now have of ever getting there? What was the point of slaying all her adversaries if she was never going to get to where she wanted to be?

Yet, despite her disappointment, she considered that now she was here she should at least make the effort to get to know these cats better. After all, at least then it wouldn't have been a *completely* wasted journey!

So, she turned to Snowy and said, 'Let's just say the Dairy *does* exist. What would you wish for if you did get there and *did* get to drink the Cream of Life?'

Snowy looked up at the sky and sighed. 'If I *did* get to drink the Cream? Well, for starters, I would give up being a show cat and get a life instead! At the moment, my days seem to merely consist of one cat show after another. I always have to look *so* perfect. I never get to just have some fun. In fact, my owners would go crazy if they knew I was out here now, sitting next to a compost heap! It's only because I knew they were out for the whole day that I dared to sneak away!'

As Snowy spoke, the other cats pricked up their ears.

'If *I* got to drink the Cream, I would wish that I was in a happy relationship,' said Smudge.

Serendipity looked at Smudge in amazement, recalling how she had often observed Smudge and Spot curled up under their favourite rhododendron bush.

'But, I thought you had a *great* relationship,' exclaimed Serendipity. 'You and your partner always look so in love!'

'Oh, that's all for show,' replied Smudge rolling her eyes. 'Our relationship is actually in *big* trouble. In fact, I'm on the verge of leaving him. He doesn't appreciate me, takes me for granted and we're constantly having rows!'

At this point, more cats began to join in.

'Well, if *I* got to drink the Cream, I would wish for a more rewarding, less stressful job,' said Ginger. 'Would you believe it, I'm expected to act as a guard cat for my owners? The pressure I'm under is ridiculous! I don't know why they don't just get a dog to do the job. It's much too much to ask of a single cat. I go to bed every night feeling uptight and stressed. This is the first afternoon I've had off in about a year! I never get to see my family or have any fun. I'm sure it will drive me to an early grave!'

Tabby then interjected. 'Well, at least you all have partners. What do you think it's like being single year after year?! I do my best to get noticed, jumping from roof to roof, performing amazing acrobatic feats – but no female cats seem to want to know! So, if *I* got to drink the Cream, I would wish for a girlfriend!'

Serendipity was amazed by what she was hearing. How could it be true what the cats were saying? When she watched them from the conservatory window, they all seemed to live perfect lives.

Yet, from what they were now saying, despite appearances, it was clear that their lives were indeed *far* from perfect.

She thought back to her first conversation with Polly, recalling how her friend had insisted that everyone had something in their lives they wanted to change.

Serendipity hadn't believed her at the time, but now, after talking to these cats, she knew it must be true!

When she thought about what she had learned from Polly about setting goals and achieving them, it occurred to her that she now had so much she could teach the other cats. In fact, it seemed they could all do with a little help!

As Serendipity pondered these thoughts, Tabby turned to her and said, 'We've all told you what *we* would wish for. So tell us Serendipity – if you got to drink the Cream, what would *you* wish for?'

Serendipity thought back to what she had said to Polly about her Wheel of Life and what it would look like if it were full.

'Well,' she began, 'first of all, I would wish that my life was filled with fun and excitement. I would wish I could wake up excited about the day ahead and have the confidence to live my life fearlessly. I would wish that I had a great social life with lots of friends, and at least one close friend I could always talk to. I would wish I was fit and healthy and lived in a nice house with a great view. I would wish I was wealthy, had a job I enjoyed and could live with a sense of purpose. I would wish I had a human family who loved me, a loving partner and a family of my own.'

When she had finished, Tabby said with a laugh, 'So . . . not much then!'

Serendipity gave an embarrassed smile. 'Well, obviously I wouldn't expect to have *all* those things from drinking the Cream, but to have most of them would be nice!' she said, recalling how she would know she had achieved her goal when three-quarters of her Wheel of Life was full.

'Still sounds a bit greedy to me!' said Ginger with a shrug.

'Let's just hope you find someone who knows where the Dairy is, as it sounds like you have quite an appetite for cream!'

As Ginger spoke, Serendipity again thought about her dream of getting to the Dairy and how it now seemed to be slipping away. She felt the fingers of Dejection begin to wrap around her throat and the hands of Regret squeezing tight as she thought about how wonderful it would have been if she had got to drink the Cream.

And then it hit her. The realisation was as shocking as it was sudden.

'*I know where the Dairy is,*' she said in no more than a whisper.

All the cats looked at her in amazement.

'What did you say?' demanded Ginger, not sure he had heard correctly.

'I know where the Dairy is!' Serendipity repeated, this time projecting her voice with more confidence, as the truth now became crystal clear.

She did indeed live a life filled with fun and excitement. She did indeed look forward to each new day and have the confidence to live her life fearlessly. She did indeed now have good friends in Polly and Mischief – and had just met a host of potential new friends. Due to her new balanced diet and exercise plan she was indeed now fit and healthy. She had indeed come to appreciate what a beautiful house she lived in and what an amazing view she now had of the world outside. She was indeed wealthy, not with money but with all the riches that life could offer. But, most importantly, she had discovered her true purpose in life, which was to help others to achieve their dreams.

Recalling what Snowy had said earlier, she realised she had indeed come a long, long way, slain many monsters, crossed raging rivers and scaled great heights. But the journey had been worthwhile, as she now knew she had reached her destination.

She was already at the Dairy. And she had drunk the Cream.

'I know where the Dairy is!' she said again and again, trying hard to suppress her excitement.

'But you just asked us if *we* knew where to find the Dairy. Why did you ask us if you already knew?' asked Ginger incredulously.

'Oh,' replied Serendipity matter-of-factly. 'I have always known, I just didn't realise it until now.'

All the cats looked at each other, shaking their heads in disbelief.

'OK then,' challenged Tabby. 'Tell us Serendipity. If you know where the Dairy is, please tell us how we get there.'

But Serendipity just smiled and, remembering something Polly had once said, knowingly replied,

'Knowledge of what is does not open the door directly to what should be.'

'What on earth does that mean?' asked Smudge, shaking her head in confusion. 'You're just talking in riddles. We need hard facts here!'

But Serendipity merely added, 'When you understand this riddle, you will know you are close to finding the Dairy.'

For Serendipity now knew exactly what the riddle meant.

To get to where you want to be, you need to find your own way there. Polly had merely been her guide – the exact route she had discovered herself. The journey would be different for everyone, yet the journey was as important as reaching your destination. The more challenging the journey, the sweeter the Cream would taste.

Serendipity looked again at the cats and saw them all shaking their heads in frustration.

'OK then, just give us a clue about where to start,' Ginger asked impatiently.

Yet Serendipity merely replied, 'Just ask yourself, *"What does happiness mean to me?"* That's a very good place to start.'

On hearing this, the cats looked at each other with even more confusion, still feeling none the wiser as to how they would get to the Dairy.

Yet Serendipity knew that, with her help, they would all get there sooner than they thought.

Looking up at the sky, Serendipity saw it was starting to get dark and realised that she had been out much longer than she had originally planned.

'Look,' she said, 'I would love to talk some more, but I have someone I need to talk to urgently. Now I know how to get here, I can come back to visit you all again and we can talk some more.'

'That would be great!' said Ginger excitedly. 'As long as you come back and help us find the Dairy!'

'Yes,' said Smudge. 'We would love you to come back again so we can all start planning our journeys to the Dairy!'

All the other cats nodded in agreement.

'Of course I will!' replied Serendipity. 'I will even draw you a map to guide you!' She then gave a wave and walked back towards the stream.

This time she felt no fear, only confidence as she crossed the stream, climbed the wall and dropped down into the garden below.

As she made her way back towards the cat flap, she considered how there were now only two sections of her Wheel of Life still empty: 'family life' and 'love life'.

Yet, that didn't really matter to Serendipity as she had achieved her goal.

Her Wheel of Life was now at least three-quarters full!

Besides, she knew she still had time to find that special tom and have a family of her own. The most important thing was that she had learned to love herself which she now knew was the greatest love of all.

She just couldn't wait to tell Polly all about what she had discovered today and her exciting plans for the future – especially her new role in helping the other cats to get to the Dairy.

She then decided to draft a map, which she knew would help

any cat who read it to find their own way there. When she had written it in her mind she felt excited at the prospect of showing it to Polly. She then bounded across the garden full of anticipation of seeing her friend again.

When Serendipity got to the end of the garden she found Mischief anxiously waiting for her.

'Hey, where have you been?' Mischief enquired, eyes wide with concern.

'Oh, just found my way to the Dairy,' Serendipity replied matter-of-factly.

Mischief looked at her incredulously. 'What?!! What do you mean *you've just found your way to the Dairy*?! Where is it and how come you went without me!?'

Serendipity merely cocked her head and replied, 'Well, I thought I would just try to get across the wall to ask the other cats if they knew where the Dairy was and, well, it ended up that I didn't need their help after all!'

'Well, don't keep me in suspense,' demanded Mischief. 'Where is it? Is it really that near by?'

'My dear Mischief,' replied Serendipity. 'It's much nearer than you think! I would love to tell you all about it but I will have to talk to you later. Right now there is someone I need to speak to urgently!'

Mischief found it hard to contain her disappointment but said reluctantly, 'OK, well, can you at least tell me if you got to drink the Cream of Life!'

Serendipity replied with a wink, 'Every last drop!'

She then made her way towards the door and shot though the cat flap. Not really caring whether her owners were in or not, she then bolted as fast as she could towards the study.

She just couldn't wait to surprise Polly with the wonderful news!

Yet, as she nudged open the study door, she was greeted to a blast of cold air that nearly knocked her off her feet.

As she regained her balance, she looked across the room and immediately noticed that something about it was different ...

The window was wide open.

And the cage was empty.

14

'Every journey has an end'[16]

Serendipity was stunned. Why was Polly not in her cage? Where had she gone and why was the window open? As she stared in disbelief at the empty cage, she suddenly remembered something Polly had once said.

'You see, I have spent my life travelling around the world helping others, just like you. Once I have helped them to achieve their dreams I move on to help someone else. I just hop out of my cage and make my way to another pet store and wait for someone else to buy me.'

And then she knew.

Polly had succeeded in helping her to find the Dairy. She had now gone off to make someone else's dreams come true.

Seeing the empty cage standing before her now, the sense of loss was overwhelming. Polly had been such a big part of her life, she just couldn't imagine not having their weekly meetings to look forward to.

As her eyes filled up with tears, the last six weeks of her life flashed before her. She remembered with shame her initial resistance to Polly's help, her petulance and her rudeness to the bird. She then recalled the growing bond of friendship she had formed with this mysterious parrot and her own transformation into the proud and confident cat she was today.

---

[16] Seneca (Roman philosopher 4 BC–65 AD).

She only wished she had had the chance to say goodbye to her friend and to thank her for all her help.

Yet, through her tears, she thought she saw something out of the corner of her eye. It was no more than a flash of colour, yet in that moment Serendipity had a realisation.

Polly may not be in her cage any more, but she would always have a place in her heart.

Wherever she was, she knew Polly would be watching over her, wishing her well and cheering her on.

Serendipity then made a pledge that Polly's legacy would always live on through her. She had learned so much from the parrot, she now felt a great responsibility to share this knowledge with others. After all, the other cats were relying on her to help them get to the Dairy. It was therefore her duty to be the best guide she could possibly be.

Thinking about her new role of helping others to achieve their dreams, Serendipity recalled the many ways in which Polly had helped her in her journey.

❧ Polly had always listened to what she had to say and had never interrupted

❧ Polly had never told her what to do – only guided her towards finding the answers for herself

❧ Polly had known exactly the right sort of questions to ask to help her find those answers

❧ Polly had never judged her – only encouraged her to be the best she could possibly be

❧ Polly had always believed in her, even when she hadn't believed in herself

❧ Polly had remained committed to helping her throughout her journey

❧ Polly had never given up on her even when she had felt like giving up on herself

As Serendipity went through this list, she realised that these were the qualities she would need to adopt if she was going to help the other cats get to the Dairy. She would need to be the inspiration to them that Polly had been to her.

Yet, she felt truly confident she could achieve this because Polly was the best role model anyone could ever have!

Serendipity was suddenly amazed at how wonderful she now felt. In fact, she felt a wave of excitement flow through her as she looked forward to the many adventures that lay ahead.

Her journey to the Dairy had just been the start of many more to come and she now knew that the only obstacles she would face were the ones inside her mind.

However, now she had the tools to overcome Procrastination, Dejection, Fear, Limiting Beliefs and Regret, she knew she could overcome anything that might lie in her path.

Yet, when she thought about the demons inside her mind, it occurred to her there was one last mystery she needed to solve.

Where on earth had all her adversaries come from?

She was sure she hadn't been born with Fear or Limiting Beliefs about herself. As a kitten she had felt invincible and had embraced each day fearlessly. As she had taken her first few steps, she hadn't felt Dejection when she had toppled over. She had just got straight back up and tried again until she could walk on all fours! She hadn't been seduced by Procrastination and put off trying to talk, just because it was hard. She had just kept going until she could make herself understood. She hadn't given up trying to drink just because the other kittens got to the milk first, and she hadn't felt any Regret because she was much smaller than them. Instead, she had naturally embraced Acceptance and made the best of what she had. She hadn't stayed clinging to her mother's coat, just because everything seemed much bigger than her. No, she had been naturally curious to discover as much about the world as she could!

So, if she hadn't been *born* with Procrastination, Dejection,

Fear, Limiting Beliefs or Regret, where had these demons come from?

As she pondered this question, it slowly dawned on her that, gradually, over time, life had just got in the way and she had learned about Rejection. And it had hurt. So, to avoid more pain, something had stopped her from trying new things. Something didn't want her to get hurt any more.

That something was her.

So, it must have been she, herself, that had created Fear, Dejection, Procrastination, Limiting Beliefs and Regret, not to cause her pain, but to protect herself from it. Yet, in trying to stop herself from getting hurt, she had denied herself the pleasure that comes from freedom, confidence and success.

When she thought about her fears in this way, she realised that their intention was *not* to stop her from achieving her goals and being happy – but to protect her from pain. So, in fact, they were really her friends, not her enemies – misguided but well-meaning friends!

But, why on earth had Polly not explained all this to her before? Why let her think her mind was full of demons out to get her?

She then clearly heard Polly's voice calling out to her from inside her mind.

'Knowledge of what is does not open the door directly to what should be.'

She then understood. If Polly had told her the truth about her fears, would she have risen to the challenges in the way that she did? Perhaps not! This had been something else she had needed to discover for herself.

Serendipity chuckled to herself as she thought about the new-found friends in her mind and the challenges they would no doubt present to her in the future! Yet, knowing they were no longer her enemies gave her a warm feeling inside.

Thinking about how she could now use her fears, she held out her paws in front of her.

On her left paw she visualised her fears and on the right paw she visualised her new found Higher Self. Realising that, in the end, they both wanted good things for her, she put her paws together to combine the resources of her fears and her Higher Self and held this to her chest. She now felt invincible!

Still caught up in this wonderful feeling, she then heard a shriek.

As she turned round to see where the noise was coming from, a little girl came rushing into the study.

'Mum, look, look, Serendipity's back!' she heard the girl exclaim excitedly.

To Serendipity's surprise, the little girl then bent down and swept her up in her arms.

'Oh Serendipity, where have you been?' the little girl exclaimed. 'We've been *so* worried about you. Never, ever go off like that again!'

Serendipity was stunned. Why was the little girl suddenly being so friendly to her?!

Just as she was trying to make sense of this unexpected show of affection, in walked the girl's mother.

Yet to her surprise, the mother too rushed up to Serendipity and began stroking her gently on her head.

'Oh, Serendipity, we thought we had lost you as well. First, that wretched parrot escapes out of its cage and then you go missing! Not that we minded seeing the back of that parrot. It was totally useless! It never said a word – just sat and stared at us all day! But you are such a *beautiful* cat and have been part of the family for so long – we would have been lost without you!'

Serendipity was amazed by what the mother was saying. She never thought she would hear her owners say such wonderful things about her! Had they always loved her this much but she just hadn't noticed? Had she just been *assuming* they didn't appreciate her all this time?

'*Perception is not always reality, my dear Serendipity, perception is not always reality!*' she heard a little voice say somewhere in the back of her mind.

Serendipity then realised with glee that another section of her Wheel of Life had just been filled.

She may not have her real cat family any more but she now knew she did indeed have a human family who loved and cared for her – and for that she was truly grateful.

It occurred to her now there was only one section of her Wheel of Life still left empty.

That section was 'love life'.

However, it rather seemed like that particular section would just have to wait for now.

As Serendipity relaxed in the little girl's arms, she was taken out into the pantry.

'Look, Serendipity! Look who we found waiting outside the door!' the little girl exclaimed excitedly.

As the girl put her down on the pantry floor, Serendipity came face to face with Mischief who was grinning from ear to ear.

And with Mischief was another cat.

But she had *never* seen this cat before.

This cat was the biggest, blackest, sleekest tom she had ever set eyes on.

And he was looking straight at her with a big smile of his face!

'Hey kiddo,' said Mischief with an equally big grin. 'This is my new mate Smokey. I've just discovered he lives next door. Thought you might like to meet him!'

The tom then said with a smile, 'I don't mean to intrude on

you but, as Mischief said, I live right next door. I couldn't help but notice you in the garden doing your exercises each day. You are such a beautiful cat I really wanted to get to know you better.'

Serendipity was once again amazed. Did this gorgeous tom really want to get to know *her* better?!

'Well, thank you very much!' Serendipity replied with a smile. 'It would be great to get to know *you* better too! My name's Serendipity.'

Smokey's eyes widened. '*The* Serendipity? Wow, I've heard so much about you from the other cats in the lane. Not only are you beautiful, you are clearly courageous too. I've heard all about your many adventures. I even heard that you know how to get to the Dairy!'

'Well, yes, that's right,' replied Serendipity confidently. 'I do *indeed* know where the Dairy is. I could even show you how to get there!'

'Wow!' exclaimed Smokey. 'Thank goodness I found the courage to come in and talk to you. It would indeed be wonderful to get to the Dairy and to drink the Cream. If I did, then the first thing I would wish for would be to find a beautiful cat to share my life with. I've been single far too long.'

With that, Serendipity smiled and said, 'You know, I'm sure I can help you achieve your goal. Maybe we should make a regular time each week to get together to help you plan your journey.'

'Sounds like an excellent idea,' said Smokey enthusiastically, as Mischief looked on with encouragement.

'I wouldn't mind getting to the Dairy myself,' added Mischief excitedly.

'Not a problem!' replied Serendipity with a huge grin.

Just then the door opened and in walked the little girl's mother with a large bowl in her hand.

'You know, it's so good to have you back Serendipity,' she said. 'I've brought you a nice bowl of cream to help us celebrate. Maybe you would like to share it with your friends. It's from the new dairy that has just opened down the road!'

Serendipity laughed as she looked at the bowl of cream, which looked delicious.

'Would you care to join me in a bowl of cream?' she asked, looking at Smokey and Mischief.

'I would be delighted!' Smokey replied.

'You bet!' exclaimed Mischief.

And all three began to drink from the bowl.

And it *did indeed* taste delicious.

As she drank, Serendipity reflected on how glad she was that she had made that very first step to leave her comfortable warm basket. That first step had led her to many, many more steps. Those first few steps had been hard but then, as if by magic, everything had just seemed to fall into place.

Like a ship on the ocean, once she had set her course and set sail, it seemed as if the universe had conspired to lead her to exactly where she wanted to be. She had set out looking for the Dairy yet somehow, along the way, she had ended up finding so much more.

She recalled a saying she had once heard as a kitten: *'A ship in harbour is safe – but that's not what ships are built for.'*[17]

She now understood exactly what it meant.

She had an amazing life to live and a destiny to fulfil.

'Tell me,' said Smokey, as he paused from drinking. 'Serendipity is such a beautiful name. Do you know what it means?'

'I'm not sure,' she replied, thinking back to what Polly had said to her when they had first met.

---

[17] John A. Shedd, *Salt from my Attic* (1928).

'Your name means something very special. You will find out its meaning when the time is right ... and you will know exactly when that time has come.'

As she pondered these words, she heard a thud.

A gust of wind had knocked off one of the books from the shelf above, missing Serendipity's head by a mere whisker.

Looking down at the book lying open on the floor she could see it was a dictionary.

And it was open at words beginning with 'S'.

And the first word on the page was SERENDIPITY.

> Serendipity 'n': The happy knack of making unexpected and delightful discoveries, often whilst searching for something else.

As Serendipity looked over at Smokey drinking greedily from the bowl, she smiled and thought to herself with pride, *Now, I really do feel like... The cat that got the Cream!*

15

Your own Journey to the Celestial Dairy

Hello! Polly here!!

You have already followed Serendipity's journey to the Dairy and you are now ready to begin your own exciting adventure!

It is my job to guide you through the steps you will need to take to discover your dreams and to make them come true.

Step 1: Acknowledge what needs to change

Remember, 'You can't change what you don't acknowledge!' The fact that you are reading this now may indicate you have already acknowledged there is something about your life that you would like to change. This means you have already taken the first step in your journey!

Step 2: Dare to dream

Remember, 'If you don't have a dream, then you can't have a dream come true!'

To help you with this step, try the following exercises:

1. Ask yourself: what does *happiness* mean to me?

2. Think of a time when you were most happy and felt most

fulfilled. Where were you? What were you doing? Who were you with? What exactly were you feeling?

3. Make a list of all the things you have ever wanted to do, all the things you have ever wanted to have and all the things you have ever wanted to be. Let your imagination run wild in order to open the floodgates of your subconscious mind. Do this exercise over a couple of days to give yourself plenty of time to really explore these ideas in detail.

4. *The rocking-chair test.* Imagine you are about to meet your maker. You have reached a ripe old age and you are sitting in your rocking chair reflecting on the wonderful life you have led. Write out in as much detail as you can all the things you would like to have done and all the things you would like to have achieved. Reflect on how you feel when you look back over this truly fulfilled life. In contrast, think about how would you feel if you looked back over your life and had *never* achieved these things.

5. *Your funeral speech.* Imagine it is your funeral and someone is about to write a speech all about *you.* Think about what you would like them to say about you and then write out the speech in as much detail as you can. Then, reflect on how you would feel when you hear these wonderful things said about you.

Now, look back at what you have written in the previous five exercises.

Then ask yourself; *Why* do I want to have these things? *Why* do I want to do these things? *Why* would I want to be this person? *Why* would I want someone to say these things about me? *Why* are these things important to me?

After all, establishing '*why*' you want something is as important as deciding '*how*' you are going to achieve it!

If you can't come up with a good reason *why* you want to

have these things and acquire these qualities, then it is probably because having them wouldn't be compatible with your core values.

What are your values?

Your values are things that are personal to you. They tell you about who you are and what is important to you. They are what you *should* be getting up for in the morning! Honouring your values is an important step to achieving happiness and fulfilment in your life.

Everyone has a unique set of values that will shape every aspect of their lives. Before you set any goals, it is important to be really clear about what these values are. To help you identify your core values, look back over the previous exercises. From the answers you gave, highlight the qualities and principles you value in yourself and others, your life and the world around you.

If you are still not sure about what your core values are, ask yourself the following specific questions:

* What qualities would you like to have?
* How would you like other people to see you?
* What qualities would you look for in a friend or partner?
* What qualities do you admire in other people or those you look up to?
* If you were given lots of power, how would you like to use it?

Keep your list of values for future reference. It is these values that you will need to honour if you are going to find true happiness from achieving your goals.

To further reinforce what is important to you, think of some times in your life when you were most *unhappy* and felt most *unfulfilled*. How did you feel and what was happening that made you feel like this? What would you *not* want people to say about you in your funeral speech? The answers to these questions should directly oppose your true values and serve to reinforce exactly what is important to you and why.

Step 3: Decide what you want

The previous exercises will give you a broad idea about what you want out of life and what will contribute most to your future happiness. However, if you are going to make real long lasting changes to your life, you need to get specific about what it is that is *most* important to you.

To do this, you will need to break down you life into sections. We, in the trade, call this your Wheel of Life!

Start by identifying some key areas of your life.

Suggestions are as follows:

* Physical environment
* Social life
* Recreation/hobbies/interests
* Family life
* Physical well-being/health and fitness
* Emotional/spiritual well-being
* Personal development
* Love life
* Career
* Financial situation

Then, draw a circle and divide it up into sections to represent the key areas you have highlighted. Write out in detail how you would ideally like each area of your life to be.

Step 4: Identify the gap between dream and reality

You will now need to compare your ideal life with your current situation. To do this, mark along each spoke of the wheel with ten equal divisions, numbering them from 1 in the centre to 10 on the circumference. Then, give each area of your life a score out of 10 for current level of satisfaction. Draw a line from one spoke to the next, linked to the score for each section. This will give you a new outline for your circle and will, at a glance, give you an idea of where your life is out of balance.

Now look at each section and think about *why* you would like that section to be full. Would acquiring these things be in line with your core values and how much would they contribute to your overall happiness? Next, decide how important you feel each section is for achieving happiness.

You now need to decide which areas of your life need most attention. Remember to weigh up how full each section currently is with how important you feel that section is for achieving happiness in your life.

Step 5: Set some smart goals

When you have decided which areas of your life need most attention, you need to get really specific about what you want. You do this by setting some *goals*. You can work on more than one area of your life at a time but be careful not to overload yourself with too many goals. Four or five goals should be sufficient.

There are four types of goal:

* Ongoing goals (such as eating healthily), which need daily input
* Short-term goals (such as catching up with friends) which may be achieved within a week to a month

* Medium-term goals (such as reaching a target weight), usually achieved within a month to a year
* Long-term goals (such as changing career or relocating), usually taking a year or more to complete

Remember, when setting goals, always state them in the positive. For example:

Stated in the negative: to *not* be *overweight*
Stated in the positive: to be slimmer

When setting goals, also remember to make them SMART

Specific

This means you should know *exactly* what you want to achieve from your goal.

Non-specific goal: To be a bit slimmer
Specific goal   To reach target weight of X

Measurable

Being *measurable* means you are able to define *exactly* what success means to you. After all, 'what gets measured, gets done!' Goals stated in units of time, weight, or currency are generally the easiest to measure. However, if you can't measure your goal in this way, define *exactly* what will be happening when you have achieved your goal.

Ambitious

In order to be really motivated to achieve your goal, you need to be able to get really *excited* about it. We have already seen there are several types of goal – so make sure at least some are big and ambitious! After all, the bigger the goal, the more exciting the outcome is likely to be! The more exciting the outcome, the more likely you are to take the required actions to achieve it. To help you get really excited about achieving your goal, try visualising the outcome in detail. Imagine what you will be doing, what you will be seeing, what you will be hearing and what you will be feeling. Do this regularly, at least once a day, to help keep you feeling really motivated!

At this point, I would mention that the 'A' in SMART is often referred to as standing for 'attainable'. However, I feel this is covered in the next section – 'realistic'.

Realistic

While keeping your goals bold and ambitious, make sure they are ones you truly believe you can attain. However, always be open-minded when taking advice from other people. Some people will be well-meaning and give good advice, while others may not necessarily be so! Remember, it's what *you* believe is realistic that really counts.

Time-specific

A goal is a dream with a date! So, when exactly do you expect to achieve your goals? Having a specific deadline for your goals will keep you motivated and encourage you to take the required actions to achieve them. However, think carefully when setting deadlines. Make the deadline too tight and you risk overloading yourself; too far in the future and you risk losing sight of your goal. So, make sure the deadline is realistic but also challenging!

When you have set your goal or goals, check again that they are compatible with your core values. Ask yourself if achieving these things will *really* contribute to increasing your future happiness and why.

Step 6: Identify current resources and potential obstacles

Look again at your Wheel of Life and identify what is good that is happening right now. This will give you an idea of the resources you currently have available to help you to achieve your goals.

Then ask yourself the following questions:

* What have I done so far to make things the way I want them to be?
* What stopped me from doing more?
* What might stop me now from achieving my goals?
* What can I do to overcome these obstacles?
* What resources do I currently have that could help me?
* What further resources might I need?

Step 7: Identify possible options

It's now time to brainstorm all the possible options available to help you to achieve your goal or goals.

If you are stuck for things you could do to take you forward, try asking the following questions:

* What would I do if money wasn't an issue?
* What would I do if time wasn't a factor?
* What would I do if I knew I couldn't fail?
* What would I do if I didn't have to live with the consequences?

These questions allow you to be creative and will free up your subconscious mind to explore a wealth of possibilities – without the restrictions imposed by your conscious mind.

Although some ideas may not on the face of it seem 'realistic', they may kick-start other ideas which you *do* feel you could use.

Step 8: Put together an action plan and timetable

You now need to decide what specific actions you are going to take from your list of options. Begin by identifying the easiest and most straightforward. These will be the ones that you will need to do first.

Make a list of the actions you are going to take in the next week and decide *when* specifically you are going to do them. Then ask yourself:

What is my level of commitment to these actions on a scale of 1–10?

If this figure is not 10 out of 10, what stops it from being 10? Then ask yourself, 'What will happen if I don't take this action?' This question usually has the effect of dramatically increasing your level of commitment!

Now it's time to make a *long-term* action plan for achieving your goal or goals.

Serendipity's goal was over a six-week period but, as we have seen, some goals may be over several months or even years. If your goal is to be achieved over a short period, write down what you hope to achieve each week; if it is over a year, write down what you hope to achieve each month; if it is over several years, write down what you hope to achieve each year and what you hope to achieve each month of the first year. Breaking your goals down into bite-sized chunks will help make the task seem more achievable.

You now have your long-term action plan!

At the beginning of each week write down the actions you will need to take that week and which day you will take each action. Every morning, review the actions you are to take that day.

It is important to look at your goals and action plan regularly and, if necessary, update the actions and timescales. I suggest you look at your goals and action plan first thing in the morning and last thing in the evening. Even better, carry them around with you so they are available to you throughout the day!

To keep yourself focused and motivated, regularly visualise yourself achieving your goal. Make the image as vivid as possible, make the sounds loud, the colours bright and the feelings really strong.

Next, make a movie in your mind of your journey towards reaching your goal, visualising the steps you will need to take. This will help programme your mind for success!

Step 9: You are now ready to take *action*!

Step 10: Prepare to overcome possible obstacles

i) Procrastination

Often, just the thought of taking a specific action will produce discomfort as it requires you to get out of your comfort zone. It is then tempting to give into inaction. While inaction may well give you a temporary feeling of relief, this is usually short-lived and will be quickly replaced with feelings of disappointment and frustration. The longer actions are put off, the more opportunities are lost and the greater the feelings of disappointment will be.

This is demonstrated by the vicious circle created by inaction:

Thought of taking action (discomfort) ... inaction (temporary relief from discomfort) ... feelings of failure and regret (greater discomfort) ... thought of taking action (even greater discomfort due to time lapse) ... inaction (feelings of relief stronger than before) ... feelings of failure and regret (even greater than before) ... thought of taking action (more discomfort due to even greater time lapse) ... opportunities lost or actions abandoned.

When you feel procrastination tempting you with inaction, you need to call upon motivation. This will help break the vicious circle of inaction and replace it with the circle of action:

Thought of taking action (discomfort) ... overcome inaction by creating motivation ... take action (feel good) ... thought of taking more action (less discomfort) ... take more action ... (feel great) ... thought of taking more action (feel comfortable) ... take more action (feel amazing) ... thought of taking more action (exciting) ... take more action ... goals achieved!!

Motivation is the incentive to get things done.

You get things done by thinking about the good things that will happen if you *do* take action (carrot) or the negative things that will happen if you *don't* take action (stick).

To call upon motivation, try the following:

Ask some power questions

* What *will* happen if I *do* take action?
* What *will* happen if I *don't* take action?
* What *won't* happen if I *do* take action?
* What *won't* happen if I *don't* take action?

These questions will get you to think about the benefits of taking action compared with the disadvantages of inaction. When you ask these questions, think about the long-term consequences as well as the short-term consequences of each outcome.

Which is the most powerful motivator for you? Is it the carrot or the stick? Finding out what motivates you is an important step to finding the tools to beat procrastination!

Create an anchor

Another way to find motivation is to create an *anchor*. This is a technique that will help programme your brain to associate a feeling with a specific action.

Firstly, think of a time when you felt really motivated. Picture what you were doing, what you were seeing, hearing and feeling. When the feelings of motivation are at their strongest, press your thumb and forefinger together. Do this several times to really build up the association. Next, while still squeezing your thumb and forefinger together and holding onto the strong feelings of motivation, imagine yourself taking the required action. Say to yourself, 'Go for it!'

The more you do this, the more you will associate the feelings of motivation with the required action. You can then trigger your motivation anchor when you need to call upon motivation. When you have motivation, you will want to take action!

Once you have started taking action, it is important you keep up the momentum. Never create 'exceptions' as excuses not to take action.

Remember, Polly says, 'There are no such things as exceptions! Exceptions kill momentum!'

Once you have lost momentum, you risk losing motivation and will again be vulnerable to procrastination.

To keep hold of momentum and motivation, make a note of

your achievements each day and remember to celebrate your successes!

This could be a simple tick box like this, where you add a tick for each action completed per day.

	Mon	Tues	Weds	Thurs	Fri	Sat	Sun
Goal 1		✓✓	✓✓	✓✓✓		✓✓✓	✓✓✓
Goal 2			✓	✓✓✓			
Goal 3		✓✓	✓✓		✓✓		
Goal 4	✓✓						

ii) Dejection

Sometimes, even when you take action, you don't always get the results that you want. This is when you can meet dejection. Dejection can make you feel so bad it can prevent you from taking further action. To combat dejection, you need to call upon resilience. You do this by asking some power questions. However, avoid asking 'Why?' questions which often focus on the problem. For example, instead of asking '*Why* did I fail?' ask yourself some 'What?' questions which instead focus on *solutions*:

* What stopped me getting what I want?
* What can I learn from what happened?
* What can I do differently next time?
* What's good about what has happened?
* What else is good that is happening in my life right now?
* What else can I do to make things the way I want them to be?
* What can I do to enjoy the process towards getting what I want?

When you ask yourself these questions, you are encouraged to see the *opportunities* rather than the obstacles in your way.

This gives you the motivation to try again in a different way and also to enjoy the process towards getting what you want!

iii) Fear

When you prepare to take action, you can often encounter fear. Fear can also stop you taking action. To overcome fear, you need to call upon courage.

You can do this by asking the following questions:

* What *will* happen if I *do* take action?
* What *won't* happen if I *do* take action?
* What *will* happen if I *don't* take action?
* What *won't* happen if I *don't* take action?

These questions will provide you with the motivation to overcome your fear and to take the required action.

You can also create a confidence anchor in the same way that you created a motivation anchor.

To do this, think of a time when you felt truly confident. Imagine what you were doing, what you were seeing, hearing and feeling. When your feelings of confidence are at their strongest, press your thumb and forefinger together. Do this several times to perfect the technique and build up the association. Next, while still squeezing your thumb and forefinger together and holding onto the strong feelings of confidence, picture yourself taking the required action. Say to yourself, 'I am now truly confident!'

The more you do this, the more you will associate the feelings of confidence with the required action. You can then trigger your confidence anchor whenever you need to call upon courage. When you have courage, you will feel able to take action!

iv) The limiting belief

Beliefs are powerful. They can affect the way you think and the way you behave. You can have beliefs about yourself, your life, other people and the world around you.

A limiting belief will hinder your progress towards reaching your goals. However, an expanding belief will *help* you in your journey.

Beliefs start off as vague ideas. A vague idea becomes a belief when you have enough evidence.

Evidence can come from the world around you, what other people say, what other people do, what you see, what you hear and what you feel. Beliefs, particularly about ourselves, are often established during childhood and can therefore be very deep-rooted.

A belief is something you no longer question. When you strongly believe something, you will either *consciously* ignore or *subconsciously* filter out evidence that might contradict that belief.

Think about your own beliefs. What beliefs do you have that could get in the way of achieving your goals? What new beliefs would you need to adopt to *help* you to reach your goals?

Once you have decided what beliefs would be helpful, you will need to *consciously* start looking for evidence to support them. Make a list of all the evidence you already have and will need to find in order to make the beliefs rock solid. To provide your *subconscious* mind with plenty of evidence, make a list of affirmations you can practise daily.

An affirmation is something you say to yourself to help programme your subconscious mind to believe it. Affirmations can be said out loud or, preferably, to yourself. Affirmations should:

* Be personal to you
* Use the word 'I'

213

* Be stated in the positive
* Be stated in the present tense
* Be short and to the point

Examples of some affirmations are as follows:

* I am a calm and confident person
* I am liked and respected by everyone I meet
* I am a positive person who seeks out opportunities
* I am a highly motivated person who takes immediate action
* I exercise with ease and am fit and healthy

Write these down and put them somewhere you can see them regularly. If at first your affirmations seem a little 'unbelievable' to you, try adding the words, 'I choose to . . . ' or 'I choose to be . . . '

After all, to a great extent we create our own reality through our thoughts and our words – so make sure you choose these wisely!

v) Regret

Regret most often appears when you give in to inaction. However, regret can appear even when you *do* take action. Regret can stop you enjoying your success and even prevent you from taking further action.

To deal with regret you first need to call upon acceptance. You do this by accepting that what is done is done, and the past cannot be changed. You then need to ask some power questions:

* What is good that is happening right now?
* What can I learn from what happened in the past?
* How can I use what I have learned to make things even better in the future?

✿ How can I enjoy the process towards making things better?

By asking these questions, you will begin to realise that, even though you *can't* change what has happened in the past, you *can* use what you have learned from the past to make things better in the future – and to enjoy yourself in the process!

***

Well, that's it folks! I now feel confident that you have the tools to enable you to achieve your goals, achieve lasting happiness and also to enjoy the journey. On the next page is a map to the Celestial Dairy that will help you to navigate your way and make sure you are always on the right track!

I must now go to help someone else achieve their dreams – so good luck! It has been great working with you!

Polly xx

***

If, after reading this book, you are now interested in receiving some personal Life Coaching, please email samantha.babington@live.co.uk

We look forward to hearing from you!

MAP TO THE CELESTIAL DAIRY

You are here!!
.
Acknowledge what needs to change
.
Dare to dream
.
Decide what you want
.
Identify the gap between dream and reality
.
Set SMART goals
.
Identify current resources and potential obstacles
.
Identify available options
.
Make an action plan and timetable
.
Take action
.
Prepare to overcome possible obstacles
Procrastination, Dejection, Fear, Limiting Beliefs, Regret
Through
Visualisation, Affirmations, Anchors, Power Questions
.
Call on **Motivation, Resilience, Courage, Expanding Beliefs,
Acceptance**
.
Take more action
.
Celebrate success
.
Produce Momentum
.
Get results
.
**Arrive at the Celestial Dairy
Drink the Cream of Life!**

Epilogue: An Uncertain Voyage

As I mentioned earlier, *Serendipity's Secret* is dedicated to my late great uncle, His Honour Judge Anthony Babington, who was a constant inspiration to me throughout my life. He never let an obstacle get in his way and was a shining example of someone who never gave into procrastination, dejection, fear, limiting beliefs or regret. Indeed, the way he conducted his life was the perfect blueprint for how to make the most of each day and to ensure that you live your life to the fullest. In fact, I would go so far as to say he was the perfect example of how to be your own life coach!

While fighting in World War II, he suffered catastrophic head injuries, which left him totally paralysed and without the power of speech. Despite being told it was highly unlikely he would ever be able to walk or speak again, he was determined to prove the doctors wrong. Fighting to overcome not only his physical injuries but also the prejudices of others, he confounded the medical profession by eventually winning back most of his powers of movement and speech. Despite numerous set-backs with his health, he eventually went on to achieve his dream of becoming a barrister and then a circuit judge.

He was also a prolific author. His autobiographies, *No Memorial* and *An Uncertain Voyage* tell the story of his incredible life's journey. I have chosen some extracts from *No Memorial* here, which I feel clearly illustrate his amazing powers of motivation, resilience, courage, expanding beliefs and acceptance.

217

Extracts from *No Memorial*
An autobiography by
Anthony Babington (1920–2004)

'Life had been scintillating, effervescent, and full of certainties. I had been strong, confident, and impregnable ... Nothing had been wasted in the past and I could look back on my life without any regrets. That life was now irretrievably ended ... '

'If I was to get better I wanted something to which I could look forward; something to be achieved, so that, if everything else in my life was to be cast aside on the rubbish-heap of "might-have beens", this, at any rate, would be an objective to which I would devote all my remaining powers ... '

'Nothing could destroy my faith in the future. It was a blind, unreasoning faith which burned within me with an unquenchable fire ... '

'One golden truth shone out in my mind: that one must get back to normality; that wounds must not make any difference; they must be accepted as a challenge and, so far as possible, they must be overcome. To me it did not seem to be a courageous thought so much as a selfish desire not to be excluded from life ... '

'The natural healing process would carry me a certain way, but beyond that, the distance I travelled would be dependent on my own effort ... '